B Martin

2-13

FOLLOWING *My* PATH

Growing Up Gay in a Christian, Fundamentalist, Right -
Wing, Conservative Family During The 1940's - 1960's

by Bernard Martin

authorHOUSE®

AuthorHouse™
1663 Liberty Drive
Bloomington, IN 47403
www.authorhouse.com
Phone: 1-800-839-8640

Published by AuthorHouse   1/4/2013

ISBN: 978-1-4772-8374-5 (sc)
ISBN: 978-1-4772-8373-8 (hc)
ISBN: 978-1-4772-8534-3 (e)

Library of Congress Control Number: 2012920232

CONTENTS

INTRODUCTION

I BELIEVE every person has a path, whether it is inherited or created, to follow as we travel the road of life. Some paths are smooth and easy. Others, like mine, are rough and bumpy, with twists and turns that can steer you off the path and guide you back again. Some paths are fairly clear; others are elusive and uncertain and sometimes even frightening. I am not sure we can even know what our true path is meant to be until we've aged considerably and have had time to reflect. It is then that we can determine whether we stayed on it or strayed off of it for a while or for always.

I am a sixty-eight-year-old, white, gay male with a legally-adopted black son. I am the grandfather of two grandchildren, both of whom I love dearly, and am a five-year cancer survivor. The cancer necessitated eleven surgeries, which ultimately left me with half a face and only one eye. I have been retired for fifteen years from the public school system as a classroom teacher, a Title I Middle School Reading teacher, a Middle School Title I Reading Program Coordinator for seventeen middle schools, and a Peer Assistance and Review (PAR) member. I am a restorer of historic homes, an antiques collector, a Christian with deep spiritual beliefs, and I am unashamed of my struggle along this rocky path to get to this point where I am now. I couldn't have said that several years ago.

The inspiration for this book came from all the people who told me that my writing is unique, forthright, and humorous. Also, five years ago, my son suggested I write a memoir. And this is what I have done. Most of my memories are as fresh as if they'd happened yesterday, but sometimes

Bernard Martin

it's a struggle to remember exactly what has happened to me during my lifetime, probably because I have repressed some of the most painful memories.

I believe everyone has a story to tell, and there are lessons to be learned from these stories. This is probably the one, major reason I have written this book; I have something I feel is important to tell so that others may learn from my experiences.

Chapter 1

EARLY CHILDHOOD

I<small>N</small> order for me to accurately describe my thoughts and feelings about growing up gay in a strict religious family, you have to know something about my family. My mother and father were married during the Great Depression and definitely understood the meaning of frugality and hard work. My mother was second generation Welch, whereas my father was English. Both believed in very large families.

My grandmother was Free Methodist, which is similar to other Holiness churches—such as Wesleyan Methodist and Nazarene Churches—in beliefs. She had twelve children; my mother was born somewhere in the middle. My grandmother took the seven girls to the Free Methodist church in a horse-drawn buggy, and my grandfather took the four boys (one died in childbirth) to the Baptist church. Sometimes they'd go fishing instead, and my grandfather told the boys not to say anything to their mother about skipping church.

My grandfather believed that girls should have a college education, whereas the boys should make their living by farming grapes, like he did. His grapes were sold to Welch's Grape Company in New York.

My mother went to college with a ten-dollar gold piece stuffed down her bosom and worked her way through Greenville Free Methodist College. My father met my mother during the last year of college. Afterward they both moved to Chicago. My Dad sold Bibles during the Depression while my mother was a nanny to children of a wealthy Chicago family on Lake Shore Drive. They saw each other only on weekends for a few short hours.

Two years later, when they had enough money saved, they were married. They then moved to New York.

I don't remember much about New York because we moved from New York to Indiana when I was only four years old. The only thing I remember is that, when I was five, Mom took me from Indiana to New York by train to see my grandmother, who had stomach cancer. My Grandmother got up out of her sick bed in the front room to make a batch of sugar cookies for me. She died four days later. She always said I was her favorite grandson. (She probably told this to every grandson!) I remember being asked to put pennies under her eyelids to keep them closed, and this frightened me. I had never seen a dead person before, let alone touched one.

Because my parents didn't believe in any form of contraception, they used the rhythm method and had six children all spaced three years apart. I was child number four, and I say it like this because that's how I felt. Both of my parents were hard workers, and as children, we didn't see them much. Mom was a stay-at-home mom, but she had a ritual that couldn't be broken: church on Sunday morning and evening, laundry on Monday, ironing on Tuesday, prayer Meeting on Wednesday nights, etc., and this routine never varied. She worked outside the home only a few times in her life. She would substitute teach, and I think she taught every child in my family at one time or another. When we came home from school, we always shared our day's experiences with each other. But because I had three older siblings, I couldn't get a word in edgewise, so I developed tics and a stutter. Mom finally took the three oldest ones aside and told them to give Bernie (me) a chance to talk whenever I opened my mouth. One of my sisters took this as favoritism, and later in life she told me she always resented that school came so easy for me; it had been difficult for her.

My early childhood memories are probably typical, but I will tell you what I remember most. I always had a prostate problem, and when I ran home from school, Mom already had the front door open so I could run straight to the bathroom. At East Wayne Elementary School in Winona Lake, Indiana, I had several happy years, although, I distinctly remember two negative things that occurred. First, I had always kissed my mother good night, but when I was around five years old, my father told me that this was no longer appropriate. My feelings were hurt, and I felt that I was doing something bad. Later, when my sister and I were both sick, my father stayed home to babysit us while my mother took the rest of the family to church. My sister and I both had our hands under the blanket because of the cold, and my dad yanked me out of the bed and spanked me and said

I had better not be "messing around with my sister." I had no idea what he was talking about, but I knew he thought I had done something bad.

Other memories are more typical of most childhoods, and they have been humorous to me in later years. There was this crazy kid, Wacky Arnold (that was his real name), in the third grade, who loved to pull my shorts down in the bathroom with one finger. (I was the littlest child in class, and Mom always dressed me in blue and white shorts, white socks, and white shoes—like the Kennedy children.) I told my sister about this, and though she was also tiny, she slid down the banister, as she always did, at recess and beat him up. This same sister told me that the dragonflies—we called them "darning needles"—that flew around our house, with no window screens and no air conditioning, would sew my eyes shut if I closed them at night. I was so frightened that I kept my eyes open all night! In the morning, I told on her, and she got spanked with a wooden spoon – my mom's favorite weapon!

Later, at the same school, I was asked to go into the hall, look at the clock there and tell Mrs. Reed, my teacher, what time it was. I didn't know how to tell time, so I ran all the way home as fast as I could and asked Mom what time it was, and then I ran all the way back and told Mrs. Reed the time. She never said anything, but the next day's lesson included how to tell time!

In the fourth grade, I stayed in after lunch for some reason one day, and my teacher had let her hair down, literally, to comb it. I told her she looked like a witch, and she replied that was not a very nice thing to say. It hurt my feelings because she was my favorite teacher. I stayed home the next day, pretending to be sick, even though my mother took our temperatures anally. This lasted three days. My mother finally called the teacher and found out the truth. I had to get out of bed and apologize to my teacher.

We played the usual cowboys and Indians, played house, and I always wanted to stay home and make the meals. My younger sister could get me to do anything. If Mom asked her to set the table, she would tell me to do it. If I didn't, she threatened to rub her eyeball with her finger—literally. And she would, as she chased me around the table. I set the table a lot!

While we went to East Wayne Elementary School, we lived in what we called the "cracker box" because it was so small for six children. It was also near the railroad tracks. We had no fear, and to this day, I shudder at some of the things we used to do. We put pennies on the tracks to flatten them out. We lay next to the tracks and dared each other to be the last one to

3

roll down the hill before a train came. We put our ears to the tracks until we could hear a train coming. One day I was angry with my parents, so I hopped a railroad car and rode down the tracks about half a mile. I got scared as it began to move faster, and rolled off and down the hill. I had to walk all the way back. If my mom only knew!

Later, we moved to the country and took a bus to school. It didn't stop at our house, but it did stop one house farther up the road, and we had to walk back. This was terrifying to me because the house where the bus stopped was a farmhouse and the owners had a goose that waited for me to get off the bus every day so it could peck at my legs as I ran all the way home. It was at least a quarter of a mile. That crazy goose never touched anybody else. I guess my bare legs were irresistible!

From first through fifth grade, I made mostly all As with some Bs, and it was an enjoyable time, except for the whippings. They were frequent, and no child was spared. The more we cried, the less we got hit with the belt in the bathroom. (I learned that early on.) But my older sister was stubborn and refused to cry and got it worse than the rest of us. I started to cry even before my dad opened the bathroom door, so I was spared more than the rest. Someone was always getting the belt from my father or the wooden spoon from my mother. My parents wholeheartedly believed that to "spare the rod" would spoil the child. Indeed, none of us were spoiled.

There were times, particularly after church, when my dad would line all of us up by age when we got home, and he would spank every one of us with his belt in the bathroom. It was like a routine. I remember one time in particular, a very prim and proper older lady sat in front of us and sneezed through her black lacey veil and then tried to blow her nose through her veil. Well, I couldn't contain my laughter, and soon we were all laughing until the minister had to stop. That was a spanking I will never forget! Sometimes, if we got too noisy in the back seat of the car, my dad would turn around and whack the first one of us he could hit! Quite often, it was me.

I also remember one regrettable time when my dad's boss died. He was a very important man, and the church was large, and the funeral was formal. My younger sister and I were to stay in the car during the funeral, and if we behaved, my mother promised we would each get a stick of gum. Karen was three, and I was six. We stayed in the car a long time, but our curiosity eventually got the best of us. Running up alongside the church, in front of a very large two-story window, was a set of iron stairs. This was during the fall, and the leaves crunched beneath our feet. Karen, who couldn't yet say Bernie, called me "Beenie Mitton" (for Bernie Martin).

She said to me, "Beenie, let's go up the stairs and see what it's like." So, she and I got out of the car and went up the stairs, leaves crunching under our feet every step of the way. When we got to the top, we could see the coffin through this very large window, and we stared in with amazement, our hands cupped over our eyes toward the window. Little did we know that we had made so much noise, the minister stopped and gazed upward toward the window. My mother's gaze followed his. She immediately rose up and came outside (by this time, we were back in the car). She didn't say a word. She just went over to a weeping willow tree, tore off a branch, and smacked us on our bare legs all the way home, which was several blocks, in front of all our friends. She didn't bother to get the car—my father was one of the pallbearers, and she knew he would bring the car home later.

We eventually moved to a farmhouse about a mile from town. Life on this small farm was different than life had been in town. But we still walked the mile or rode our bikes into Winona Lake for the day. That is, when we weren't hoeing the garden or polishing the dining-room table's legs or doing the many other tasks my mother always found for us to do.

We never had any money unless we picked mulberries and sold them by the quart in town. They were pretty squashed down after the mile-long bike ride into town, but we fluffed them up to make a whole quart. Since I was the littlest and cutest at that time, it was always my duty to knock on the doors and try to sell them while my two sisters remained in the background. Sometimes we earned a quarter or more.

We didn't have money for lunch most of the time, so we collected cans along the very busy beach and tried to sell them for enough to get a hot dog and a drink for lunch. If we were lucky, sometimes my dad picked us up in the car on the long walk home. Winona Lake, known for the Billy Sunday Tabernacle (later called the Homer Rodeheaver Tabernacle), was where we heard Billy Graham speak many times before he became famous. It was also where we listened to Homer Rodeheaver sing "How Great Thou Art." There were always Christian conferences in this area, and lots of people on the beach.

One time I met a girl on the beach who was about eighteen years old with clear, dark brown skin, beautiful white teeth, and very long hair. Her name was Laurie Maurica—she was probably Spanish—and she was from Pittsburgh. I found her every day on the beach, and I told her all about my family. I was probably six or seven at the time. I invited her home for dinner after asking Mom, and she agreed to come.

We ate at five o'clock every night, come rain or shine. We always ate well for supper and always ended it with a dessert—usually cake or pie. My mother was a good cook, and she could make a delicious mulberry pie! I told Laurie that she had to walk the mile home with me, and I assured her that I would walk her back. As we came to the country road, she took hold of my hand, and I fell instantly in love. We held hands the whole way home. I didn't realize until a little later that she only came to see my brother, who was about her same age. I was heartbroken! I wrote to her once, and she wrote back once, and that was the end of my first love affair.

On this gentleman's farm (my father knew nothing about farming, but he kept a few cows and a huge bull), the fence always needed mending to keep the cattle in. It was my job to spend the day in the field and make sure the cows didn't get out and destroy the other farmers' crops. Mom packed me a lunch, which I usually ate early in the morning, and then I would starve the rest of the day. Sometimes Karen would go with me. We were both terrified of that bull. One day we got to playing and completely forgot about the bull, which came rushing at me full-speed. I ran as fast as I could in my bare feet, just barely crawling under the fence in the nick of time and scraping my back on the barbed wire! But the bull was held at bay.

This experience reminds me of my relationship with my older brother and my other siblings. I never really knew my older brother; he was in college by the time I remember him. He never had much to do with me, and he found me to be more of a nuisance than anything. He never played with me or taught me anything. The only thing I remember about my brother was that he ran track his senior year in high school and played tennis like my dad, who had been State Champion of North Dakota in his youth.

I idolized him. One day I jumped on his bicycle when he was going somewhere so I could be with him. He pushed me off and left me on the ground and never said a thing. My feelings were hurt, and I never forgave him for that. That was just the first of many things I never forgave him for.

My two older sisters were focused on their own lives and didn't pay much attention to me. Every now and then, my second oldest sister played with my younger sister and me. This was during the era of sock hops, bobby socks, hoop skirts, skinny belts, and painted and signed corduroy pants. Shortly after this came the bell-bottom pants era. However, we were never allowed to go to any of the dances unless we skipped out of the house when my parents were extremely busy. Our parents were so strict that, even though my father owned the small town newspaper, we couldn't read it on Sunday. Nor could we study on Sunday – it was a day of rest, period. When I grew older and had a test on Monday, I had to set the alarm for midnight and then get up and study for it.

In my family, we never talked about sex—it was taboo. My father rarely showed affection toward my mother, and when he did, she played him off. I remember a time when I was about twelve years old, and my father took me for a ride out into the country. On this ride, he told me about "the birds and the bees." He was far more embarrassed than I was. After he finished speaking, for about three minutes, he asked me if I had any questions. I said, "Yes. Which do you like better, Pepsi or Coca-Cola?"

That was all that was ever said about sex. Years before, my oldest sister tried to explain how babies were made, but I cried and said I didn't believe her. I didn't think that was something my parents would ever do. I quickly dismissed it from my mind.

Then there was the time my younger sister and I went to the town's dump yard, which was midway between our house and Winona Lake. There we found everything from pornography to cigarettes, which of course we had to try. We didn't understand the pornography and left it in the dump. We decided to throw bottles at the rats and, for some reason, my sister threw a bottle at me and conked me out to unconsciousness. When I woke up, my Aunt Lillian, who shared my mother's beliefs, was standing over me praying loudly, "Dear God, don't let Bernie Jr. die." I don't know which scared me more: my aunt's prayer or the raised knot on my head!

My Aunt Lil was unique in many ways. She died in 2011 at the ripe old age of 106. Aunt Lil played an important role in our lives. She was the family matriarch, the oldest of the seven sisters, and lived a most unusual life. She became a missionary in China, but before she went, she learned to speak and write Mandarin.

She was there for only a short time when war broke out, and she marched a band of children over the mountains to safety. Soon after, she boarded a plane and returned to America. She was an avid prayer, and though she never married, she adopted all of her many nieces and nephews as her own children. And she was strict with all of them. One time while visiting us in Indiana, she baked a cake with chocolate frosting. I wanted to lick the bowl when she was finished, and she agreed to let me. But at six years of age, I couldn't wait until she was finished. She caught me in the act, and for punishment, she sat me in the corner to memorize a Bible scripture. I remember it to this day—

> "I will lift up mine eyes unto the hills, from whence cometh my help.
> My help cometh from the Lord, which made heaven and earth."
> (Psalms 121:1–2 KJV)

I have lifted my eyes unto the hills in prayer many times since.

One particularly funny story about Aunt Lil took place when she was in her early twenties. She would often pray spontaneously, right out loud, no matter where she was. One day, my mother, my aunt Lil, and another aunt were walking down the street in Chicago when a young man came upon them and snatched Aunt Lil's purse off her arm. Aunt Lil dropped to her knees and prayed loudly, "Dear Lord, help this man to understand what he has done and take away his sin." The man was so frightened that he ran back, gave her the purse, and said, "Here Ma'am, take your damn purse back."

Another funny incident was when she and her sister, my Aunt Dottie who lived with her all of her life, (both were teachers) came to Lancaster, Ohio, for a visit. She had parked her car on a rather steep hill between two Cadillacs. When they were ready to leave, Aunt Lil thought she had the car in reverse, but instead, the car crashed into the Cadillac in front of her. She then put the car in reverse, pressed down on the gas pedal, and crashed into the Cadillac behind her. And if that wasn't enough, she somehow shot across the road and hit a parked car on the other side of the street. When I came home from teaching, there was Aunt Lil, on a gurney, ready to be taken to the hospital by medics. There were people standing all around and several police cars, and the police were just standing there shaking their heads.

To make a long story even longer, Aunt Lil had broken her leg and had to stay with us for several weeks while her leg healed. She urged a policeman to give his life to Christ; he often came to visit her in the hospital, and they wrote to each other for several years afterwards. She was in her eighties when this happened! Fortunately my neighbors were understanding and didn't hold any of us responsible for the damages to their cars.

On her ninetieth birthday, the whole family got together to celebrate.

There were over a hundred people there, and money was collected to give to her as a present. Needless to say, she got quite a sum of money. When asked what she was going to do with the money, she said she would like to go to Africa. And to Africa she went—she and her sister, Aunt Dot. They even climbed to the top of Victoria Falls! Both of these aunts played an important role in all of our lives.

Chapter 2
MY FAMILY'S RELIGIOUS BELIEFS

M y family believes in God and that He sent his Son to earth to die on the cross for our sins. And if we believe this, we will go to heaven.

Most Christians believe this. But my mother took it several steps further. Her life was bound up with rules; you should not only obey the Ten Commandments, but you should also not cut your hair, if you were a woman, or wear make-up or fancy clothes or jewelry. You should do nothing more than rest on Sunday, so she would prepare Sunday dinner on Saturday evening, and then she would just put it in the oven on Sunday. She cooked no more that day.

It was up to my father to cook Sunday supper. He loved popcorn and apples, so I had popcorn and apples every Sunday before we went to evening church service. Occasionally, we could make sandwiches if there was any meat left over from Sunday's dinner.

Both of my parents showed us what hard work and frugality meant, and for this I thank them. These lessons are reflected in the lives of each of us. My oldest brother earned his doctorate in history (*summa cum laude*) from Butler University. Not many years later, he became head of the History Department at Indiana Wesleyan University. He wrote extensively and toured the around the world, delivering a talk he titled "the Christian View of World Politics." He wrote a book but died of brain cancer before it was completed. His wife and secretary completed the book and published it posthumously. He never veered from my parents' teachings.

My oldest sister, Ann, did not finish college. She married her husband,

Bob, who is adept with money, and she and her family now own and operate a large company in Elkhart, Indiana. She has lived a full life with loving children and grandchildren, and particularly with my cancer, she has been very understanding and supportive of me. Ann and her husband veered from my mother's path years ago.

My next older sister, Mary, who is closest to me in age, and her husband, Tim, both became teachers and, to my knowledge, never veered from my parent's teachings. However, there are certain topics we do not discuss.

My younger sister became a psychiatric nurse and died of brain cancer on the day she would have received her first retirement check.

My youngest brother, Marvin, became a small-town engineer, a position he has held most of his life. Ann, Karen, Marvin, and I have found our own paths to religion and to God. My mother seemed bound by a few Old Testament rules and all the New Testament rules *when they were applicable.* Those last four words are what set me apart from some of my family, especially my mother.

My mother believed in "sanctification," which was a state of grace above and beyond salvation where you tried to perfect your life to walk as close to God and Christ as possible. She felt you had to work on this your whole life. I believe it made my mother sad and, sometimes, anxious. It seemed to me she never could really enjoy her ever-evolving family; everything was taken so seriously. I never heard her crack a joke, and she would rarely smile. She did not live in the moment; she focused only on the future, when she would be called to heaven. There was no soul music, no TV, no dancing, no fun on Sunday. The preachers were mostly hellfire-and-brimstone preachers who made us feel we couldn't do enough to gain entrance into heaven, and they could lay a guilt trip on us in a second. My sisters had to wear pantyhose with seams; our fingernails had to be clean for Sunday school; we had to tithe ten percent; and we couldn't skip church for any school functions. We had to go to religious colleges for the most part.

She didn't believe in bragging, so when the names of the church members' kids who had made the honor roll were included in the church paper, ours were excluded. Nobody knew I was an A student or that my brothers and sisters were honor students. I played the piano by ear and would often play the piano or organ in church, but I had to wait until my parents were out of the house to play "Moon River" and other non-religious songs. I probably could have made a good living by playing popular music in lounges, but this was unthinkable.

I rebelled early. When I was six, I heard a sermon on "the Prodigal Son," and in Sunday school, I learned that Cain killed Abel. So I asked my mother, "If Cain killed Abel and was sent away, then whom did Cain marry, if they were the only people on earth? My Sunday school teacher also said that he brought back friends and children with him as well. Where did they come from?" Neither of my parents could answer these questions. Neither said anything about faith nor would they defend the theory of evolution, I had to believe in, as I witnessed scientific proof as I became older.

I also questioned why we followed only certain rules in the Bible, particularly Paul's writings to the churches, and not others. Again, I got no answers that satisfied me. Everything was about confessing your sins and then about sinning no more. I remember one evangelist (we had revival services for two weeks twice a year) telling the story of a man who wouldn't forsake his sins and got run over by a train on his way home and died. This scared me and sometimes prompted me to go to the altar and confess my sins. As a youngster, however, I wasn't really aware of any sins to confess, but we had to cross a railroad track on the way home, and I wasn't going to be the one who caused my family members' deaths! Another evangelist at these revivals not only preached hellfire and brimstone, but also played a carpenter's saw with a regular violin bow. Every time he played, it made me have to go to the bathroom.

These perceptions and rebellious questions bothered me throughout my life. The teachings I grew up with only perpetrated feelings of guilt and anxiety. But, as you will read, I slowly came to my own conclusions and now feel very comfortable with them.

Chapter 3
DISCOVERING THERE WAS SOMETHING DIFFERENT ABOUT ME

WHEN I was about six years old, I began to have some slightly erotic dreams. However, the subjects of my dreams were always the same gender as me. I never told anyone. As I got older, the same-gender feelings became stronger and stronger.

When I was in sixth grade, I remember sitting on the gym bleachers and hearing the boys in my class *ooh* and *aah* over the cheerleaders' legs. I felt nothing. But deep down inside, I had the same feelings when the boys' basketball team came out onto the floor. At that age, I could always pick out the best-looking male student in class, and I always wanted to sit with or be near him.

It was in the seventh grade that I had my first problem. I didn't feel comfortable taking showers in the boys' locker room after gym class. So, I forged a note with my parents' signatures stating that I had health problems that prohibited me from taking gym class. I was so paranoid that students would discover my problem and start to tease me or, even worse, pick fights with me. So I made up my mind to be such a good student academically that they might leave me alone. That same note worked for me all through high school—except when my parents found out about it. Somehow, I explained it away.

Now, when I use the word "problem," please understand that, at the time, it was the only word I knew. The term "gay" was way down the road. The closest word that came to my hearing was "pervert." But that had a terrible connotation to it. I wasn't sure what it meant anyway.

I finally heard the term "queer" and kind of figured out what it meant, but I was unwilling to accept it as a definition of me as well.

One night I ejaculated quite by chance and felt very disturbed. First, I thought I had broken one of my body's inner tubes. Then I recalled Ann's attempt at explaining how babies were born, and I became concerned that maybe I had used up one of my children. If I were to have only one child, and I had already used it up, I wouldn't be able to have any more. I speculated that maybe God had made a mistake. But then, I knew that God didn't make mistakes. I was afraid I was the only one in the world with this problem, and so I decided to will my body to science when I died. I wrote a note to that effect, signed and folded it, and have no idea what became of it. I knew I couldn't talk to my parents about this problem, nor could I talk to any of my older siblings, as they might make fun of me or, worse, tell my parents.

I became a master of deceit and kept my feelings and desires from everybody. When I saw someone on television I was attracted to (we were allowed to watch TV at my aunt's house on some holidays), I kept it to myself. I daydreamed a lot. I wasn't attracted to children, but to older, eighteen- to twenty-year-old men. My self-esteem plummeted, and I studied harder than ever. Nevertheless, my grades suffered slightly during this time of my life.

I was an avid reader, so I went to the library and discovered a book on human anatomy. It was definitely an adult book, but I sneaked it out anyway. To conceal it, I put it on the shelf with many other books when I got home. It had nothing in it to explain my problem. And of course, my mom found it and questioned me about it. I lied and denied knowing anything about the book. I don't know if the book ever made its way back to the library or not.

Finally, at about the age of eight, I stood in front of a mirror and said, "You're a queer." Then I broke down and sobbed the way I am right now as I write this—because of the pain it caused me back then. The memory of it is still so very real today. And it was so unnecessary. This book is harder to write than I had imagined!

Chapter 4
BECOMING SEXUALLY ACTIVE

I HAD decided that I couldn't be the only "queer" on this planet, so I resolved to set out and find another one. I will use the term "gay" from here on because, for me, it has a more pleasant sound and feeling to it. I must have been very sexually inquisitive early in my life because the thought of being gay continually obsessed me. It became all-consuming.

When I entered the seventh grade, we moved to Marion, Indiana, the biggest city we had ever lived in. By this time, my oldest brother and both of my sisters were married. For a while, we went to a large Wesleyan Methodist church that was connected to the college. I attended the fairly large Washington Junior High School, where once again I made good grades.

But how does one go about searching for another gay person in this era? I felt like I was in love with half of the seventh- and eighth-grade boys. Although, looking back, I think I merely wanted affection, as I wasn't getting much at home. My father made us start working at very early ages. We helped print newspapers, ran automated laundries, (including ironing), picked strawberries, took care of our family's garden, and sometimes even corded wood.

Soon, my parents travelled to Elkhart, Indiana, to work in a small Wesleyan Methodist church that was just getting started. There my parents felt they could do more good than in a large church. We traveled to Elkhart on Saturday and stayed in a cold trailer overnight. We got up early on Sunday morning and knocked on doors to invite people to the worship service.

I hated this time in my life, especially knocking on stranger's doors and inviting them to do something they didn't want to do anyway. I think my parents wanted to be missionaries, but I wondered why they had to include me. This period lasted only a short time though, and the church folded.

Marion was large enough to have a town square where cars would ride around in circles, particularly on Friday nights. When I could, I would often walk uptown and around the square searching for that elusive gay person. The first time a car stopped and a man asked me to get in, it scared me to death, but I got in anyway. I don't think we said much to each other; he was way older than I was, and he was unattractive to me as well. He drove me to a site on the fairgrounds where he fondled me. I quickly let him know that he could not do this. Instead I fondled him and massaged him to ejaculation. I wouldn't let him touch me.

He asked me how much he owed me and gave me one dollar. We never talked about what I needed to talk about. This kind of thing happened once or twice a week, depending on my schedule. I knew that I had to be home at a certain hour, so I was restricted by time. I met various guys—married men, single men, scary men, unattractive men, and all were much older than I was because I was only twelve or thirteen years old.

I had one year at Marion High School. It was a large, racially mixed high school, and fights would break out in the hallways when some student turned off the lights. Almost always, the fights were between students of different races. One African-American girl and I seemed to hit it off in Latin class, and I walked her uptown to the drugstore where we would each buy a Coke. Then we went our separate ways.

I didn't make friends with very many students at Marion, and my grades dropped slightly. And I didn't like the men who picked me up—they weren't my age and always wanted something I wasn't willing to give. I still wouldn't let them touch me. Some gave me money—sometimes quite a lot – and the others didn't. Some became upset when I wouldn't give them what they wanted and this scared me. I had never heard the term "hustler," but in hindsight, this is what I was. When they offered me money I took it, when they didn't, I never asked for any.

I felt I was killing two birds with one stone; I was meeting other people I suspected were "queers," and I was making a little money. All I knew was that I didn't want to be like any of them. As I look back on this period in my life, it's a wonder I kept it together. I could have been hurt or worse—killed. Only one younger man, who was in his early twenties, picked me up and was affectionate to me. I liked that, though I wouldn't have done it with any of the other men. Even with this younger man, I wouldn't let him touch my private parts. I did want to see him again because I felt the same about him as I had about Laurie Maurica many years earlier. But we never exchanged names or addresses, and in retrospect, he probably feared being charged with rape of a minor.

We moved from one town to another before and after Marion. I ended up going to four different high schools in four years. Before Marion we lived in Butler, then Berne, and from Berne we moved to Marion, Indiana, and then from Marion we moved to Kewanna, where I graduated from high school. Kewanna was a small town, and my senior class had fewer than thirty students. There wasn't much going on, but I did slip away occasionally to attend some of the sock hops. I actually felt safer and more comfortable in Kewanna, as there weren't any opportunities to hustle.

Berne was a Mennonite town and if you weren't Mennonite, with a name like "Neusbaum" or "Neuenshawander," or "Lehman," you weren't really accepted. Every year the Mennonite church, as well as outsiders, would perform Handel's *Messiah*. It was an outstanding performance with a 500 member choir with paid soloists. The organ was a huge pipe organ with sounds that would fill the entire enormous church. We went every year and my dad and one or two of my sisters sang in the choir for a few years.

One year, I remember distinctly, when I was about eight years old, I got very impatient during the long arias, and started to squirm and had to go to the bathroom. My mom gave me a look that told me to straighten up immediately. There was no use in asking her to go to the bathroom, so I wet my pants, and I remember the urine flowing down the pew where we were sitting. My mom took the blame for that one!

The school in Berne was interesting in that there were several Amish children who attended school until the eighth grade. There was a huge Amish settlement around Berne. They would hitch up their horses and buggies right in front of the school. I didn't get to know them as they pretty much stayed to themselves.

From Kewanna we moved to Argos, Indiana. I had already had one year of college at Olivet Nazarene College in Kankakee, Illinois, which was about a one-hour drive from Chicago. I was fortunate to get a four-year academic scholarship and worked off most of the rest of my debt by grading English papers for an English professor.

I had received my driver's license three years before moving to Argos, where my dad owned the newspaper. He often had me deliver papers during summer break to small towns around Argos, and that gave me ample excuse to explore. While in Argos during my first summer break, I drove to South Bend with quite a goal in mind. I resolved to find another gay person like myself come hell or high water. I drove directly to the bus station where cab drivers waited for customers. I walked up to one and asked him if there was a gay bar in the downtown area. I figured he would either knock me down or tell me something.

Fortunately, there was one small gay bar in the downtown area, and the cab driver told me how to get there. I had heard about gay bars from some of the newspapers I sent away for while in college. Of course I couldn't talk to anyone at Olivet; it would be just like talking to my parents. Plus Olivet, a very strict and religious college, wouldn't have understood my need-to-know anyway. We even had religious chapel services every day, where attendance was taken, and we had revivals two times a school year.

I was way underage (seventeen) when I went to my first gay bar, but to make things worse, I looked like I was fourteen. When I got to the gay bar in South Bend, I drove around the block several times until I saw an average-looking man go in. I had never been in a bar before—I hadn't even had a drink—and I didn't know what to expect. I was very underage. But I went in and ordered a Coke. Emotionally, I thought I had died and gone to heaven. These men were more like me—I was not alone after all!

I left the bar feeling better than I had ever felt. There were young men, middle-aged men, and older men. They were all friendly, and they appeared to know each other. They showed their affection for each other openly. I thought this bar had some promise—for what, I wasn't sure. But many introduced themselves to me, and I felt welcomed.

The only drawback was that, for the first time, I saw the feminine side of the gay world. I had never witnessed men who were this flamboyant, and some were extravagantly dressed. Not all were this way—actually, most weren't. I asked one kind, older man who looked like a straight professional, and he told me they were called "queens" or "sissies." And then he put his arm around me and said, "You can make a decision early in life to be one way or the other. You can learn to become "butch," or masculine, or ramp it up and be a queen. It's your decision." Later I discovered that this was not exactly true!

But, because I knew I was going to be a teacher one day, I opted for butch. I have been forever grateful to this stranger throughout my life. It took me quite some time to accept lesbians, bisexuals, cross-dressers, and gender-benders until I realized that some of the "flamers" were the ones who paved the way for the rest of us.

While I was in the bar, I was invited to a gay party. The invitation came in the mail to my home in Argos. My mother opened the letter and confronted me about my sexuality. I told her the truth and said that I was tired of lying and hiding from the truth. My mom had a hard time wrapping her head around the fact that I might be homosexual. She didn't read any books written by parents of gay children such as from PFLAG and there was no internet at this time. She only believed that God didn't want me to be this way and that doctors could fix me. My parents bought me a car, even though they didn't really have the money for it, so I could go back and forth from college to home. That was what they said. But, I knew the real reason for the car was so I could keep my appointments with a Christian psychiatrist they had found in Chicago.

After several visits to the psychiatrist, I saw I wasn't changing, and I became discouraged. By this time, I was driving to Chicago only to be part of the gay community and culture that was there.

When I was a sophomore in college, seven of us rented a home off-campus. It was for people who could be trusted. Interestingly, out of the seven, four ended up being gay, although we didn't know it about each other back then. We tried to be macho and date girls, be we intuitively knew we had each other to fall back on.

It was a very difficult schedule—going to Chicago overnight on Saturdays, studying for tests, writing term papers, and grading papers for the meager stipend I earned and needed. But I did it for the next three years and still maintained an A average. We all figured the campus was rife with gays, but we didn't talk about it much and it wasn't easy to positively identify them. I wasn't very sexually active, except when I went to Chicago. I loved the Chicago bars and the area they were mostly in—Old Town. It was kind of like a gay community with gay restaurants and bars with certain themes. I saw my first drag show there.

One Sunday, I was in this area in my car when two Mexicans jumped in on either side and shoved me to the middle of the car. Coming from a small town, I didn't lock my car doors. One had a gun; the other had a knife. I told them to take the car and let me go. They drove around for awhile, talking in Spanish, and then they stole my wallet and wanted my ring. I talked them out of taking my ring because it was engraved with my name and could be easily traced. After threatening to kill me, they dumped me beside the Chicago River. I felt like I was in a bad nightmare but happy to be released, even though I had lost my car.

Fortunately, I had just enough money to call home, and I begged my parents to come and get me. Also, fortunately, detectives traced my credit card and located the car, stripped down to the bare essentials, in some southwestern state. I identified the thieves easily in a line-up, and they received quite a long sentence due to other crimes as well.

I wasn't happy at Olivet. I knew guys who went to church every Sunday, but would talk about girls as if they were dogs. They tried to find the dirtiest movies to watch on television in the TV room; we weren't allowed to have televisions in our own rooms! And they harassed one student—a Catholic guy from the city—by stealing his clothes while he was showering and then making him walk down the hall naked while they poked fun at him. I saw a lot of hypocrisy at Olivet, and it helped form my current religious beliefs.

After my sophomore year in college, a girl, who attended the same church and college as I did, agreed that neither of us wanted to go back to Olivet. I wanted to go to a state college, which would be more affordable, and I might meet some gay people there. My friend was just tired of studying and wanted to take a year off. So, we told everyone in the church that we were not returning to Olivet the coming year. My parents said nothing. But two days before it was time for school to start, I noticed my mom washing all of my clothes. On the day it was time to return for the fall semester, my parents still said nothing, but they packed my suitcases, put them in the car, and told me to get in the car in a tone of voice I dared not disobey. They picked up the girl I knew from church, and we both were driven to Olivet. My parents dropped me off on some dormitory steps and left me. I don't know where they dropped off my friend. I sat there for two hours and decided to make the best of it.

In hindsight, I think they made the right decision for me. I got a good liberal arts degree, the professors were strict, and I learned a lot. Roll was taken in every class, and we began each class with prayer. I've always been thankful for my strict education. I graduated magna cum laude and made *Who's Who in American Universities and Colleges*. My friend became a teacher and I've never heard anything from her.

Chapter 5
AFTER COLLEGE LIFE

A FTER college, I settled into a large apartment complex in a northwest suburb of Chicago near O'Hare Airport with two other students who I found out my senior year were gay also. I had a teaching job at a very large high school. I was twenty-one, and some of my students were nineteen. I taught two college preparatory classes and the rest were a mix of everything else. There was one principal and two vice-principals. The area that the students came from was wealthy. I hated every minute of it.

I also worked at Carson, Pirie, Scott and Company (aka Carson's) in the evenings and on Saturdays. I got a letter from Norm, one of my younger sister's old boyfriends. He taught at the Iowa School for the Deaf. He acknowledged that he had always loved me and wanted to come to Chicago. Rent was very expensive, but we could share a bedroom. I had always had a thing for him, and it was instant love—for me anyway.

He was Norwegian and tall with blond hair and blue eyes. We had worked together at a mental hospital during the summer between college years. But my "gaydar" wasn't very good then, and I never suspected him of being gay.

He came to Chicago, but I never felt he really loved me. After limping along in the relationship for three years, he told me he had been unfaithful and didn't intend to stop having sex with others.

I felt hurt, sad, and hopeless. I felt trapped, too; I couldn't concentrate on teaching and sure couldn't sleep in the same bed with my cheating lover. I didn't have anywhere else to go, and neither did he because we all shared the rent. I quit my teaching job—just walked out of the classroom in the middle of the day and decided that night to commit suicide. I overdosed on some prescription drugs that put me in a coma for a week.

When I came out of the coma in a hospital with my mother standing over me, I was angry that I was still alive. I was placed in a mental institution for observation in a downtown Chicago mental hospital. This place scared the wits out of me! There were drug addicts who were talking to themselves, paranoid and schizophrenic people who would stare at you or touch you, and I had to share a room with a seriously mentally ill person who scared me to death. There were bars on every window.

I figured I wouldn't last long in this place. I discovered a public telephone and called my parents collect in Indiana and begged them to come get me. I told them if they didn't, I would find my own way out. They drove up to Chicago, and when they saw the condition of the place, they immediately pulled me out.

I was beginning to feel that being gay was dragging me down a long and lonely road. My parents decided to send me to see a Christian psychiatrist in California, where my uncle lived and my sister was attending college. He claimed he could make gay people straight. The building was large and aseptic. I went to the first session, and the psychiatrist put the make on me; I never went back, but instead, I walked the beaches of California, waiting for my sister's semester to end. Then we both took the plane back to Indiana.

I got lots of sleep for the next three months and tried hard to convince my parents that I was always going to be gay. I also told my mother that I felt I was a Christian and prayed. But she couldn't accept me as I was. My dad's only comment was, "Now you can become a real man."

My parents prayed and prayed over me. In desperation, I sent my resume to Columbus, Ohio, and I was accepted to teach in an all-black middle school. I stayed for fifteen years. I was finished with Chicago anyway. It was too big—you could go to the same bar every night and never see the same people.

The bars were the only places to meet other gay people back then. They were often raided too. That meant the police came with their hatchets, broke all the front windows out, and handcuffed as many people as they could. Then they took them away in paddy wagons. Names and addresses were printed in the *Chicago Tribune* the next day, and people were fired from their jobs and often were exiled from their communities. I saw this over and over.

One night, the lesbian daughter of a very prominent politician warned the bartenders that the bar was going to be raided that night. That didn't stop the thousand or so people from dancing the night away! The police did come and broke all the front glass. I waited in the back while hundreds were handcuffed and taken to the paddy wagons lined up in front of the bar. And then, when there was a lull, I scurried through one of the broken windows and ran to my car. It was winter, and the cold reminded me that I had left my winter coat in the bar. I waited until everything settled down, when the police cars and the paddy wagons were all gone, and I jumped through one of the broken windows and retrieved my coat. After I left Chicago, I never went back!

Chapter 6
SECOND LOVER, NEW START, AND FOND MEMORIES

I was introduced to Gary Oliver through a mutual friend. Gary was Swedish and had bright blue-green eyes and light-brown hair. He had a son, but he came home one day and found his wife in bed with another man. That was the end of their marriage. He joined the army, and after he was discharged from the army, he farmed with his father for a while in Iowa and slowly accepted that he was gay. With Gary, what you saw is what you got.

When we met, he hadn't been sexually active with a man, particularly to the degree that I had been. We were to meet at a small bar in downtown Columbus called the Cat's Meow. He said he drove around the block several times, building up his courage to come into the bar. When he did and saw me, it was love at first sight—for both of us. He belonged to the Church of Jesus Christ of Latter-day Saints. I didn't understand his religion, nor did he understand mine. But religion was never really an issue for us.

Gary came from a large farm, and he had a green thumb. He got his love of flowers from his mother. I always said he could grow a flower on a cement block without any dirt or water. Gary loved to cook, so he did most of it. I became the steady breadwinner while Gary went from job to job. We found each other to be exciting instantly. Our interests were the same, and we shared many happy memories, some of which I will relate to you.

Gary was very outgoing and knew every neighbor by the end of the week. We wanted to buy a home, and I thought I had enough money saved for a down payment. We found a traditional house with lots of character in the middle of Bexley. The suburb of Bexley, which is just east of Columbus, is kind of divided into three parts. The north part of Bexley has very expensive homes for the wealthy; the mid-Bexley homes are not inexpensive either; but the southern part of Bexley has more modest homes.

The one we found and liked was in middle Bexley. We started the buying process and were waiting for the bank to okay my credit and set a closing date. We were in love with the house and would go over and trim the hedges and mow the yard. We were even invited to the local Jewish temple. After several weeks, the bank informed us that they would not approve the loan because my teaching salary alone would not be enough money to afford the house.

We found another home in south Bexley and got it this time. It was a fairly plain, two-story traditional house that needed lots of work— painting, wallpapering, sanding the floors, etc. We threw ourselves into the remodeling immediately, painting the outside and redoing everything on the inside. We put it back on the market in nine months. We had paid seventeen thousand dollars for it, and we sold it for thirty-seven thousand dollars. The neighbors were astounded. And so were we!

We had always wanted to find an old historic home that we could live in while we restored it. The second home was just that. It was in Somerset, Ohio, which made my drive to work in Columbus fifty miles each way. This house was called the Finck Mansion and was huge. It was built by State and then U.S. Senator William E. Finck. There were three stairways, fifteen rooms, six fireplaces, five bedrooms, and tons of work to do. The house was famous in that Abraham Lincoln was supposed to have stayed the night there, as well as Henry Clay. General Sheridan, whose home is just outside of Somerset, would often visit the Fincks. We worked well together and were fast. Quite often, Gary would stay home and work on the home during the day, and I would help him in the evening after a day of teaching.

We had a family Christmas party the first year, but we had spent so much money on the house that there wasn't enough left over for essentials. I had to ask my father for money to buy toilet paper for the large group of guests. Everybody had a great time and talked about the party for years after. My mom even wrote a poem for the occasion as follows:

Somerset Saga
Or
Christmas in Ohio

The Martin's Christmas in '72
Will feature something very new.
Instead of 229 N. Michigan Street,
It's Somerset, Ohio, where we'll all meet.

It's Sheridan's hometown, General Phil, you know.
Turn by his statue to North High and go.
The house is unnumbered - never mind,
The iron picket is easy to find.

The windows agleam with candlelight
Assure questing travelers this house is right,
and the curling smoke from the chimney wide
Proclaims festivity awaits inside

The old brick house with the welcoming door
Affords many features to explore;
The big wide rooms and three stairways
Will challenge the children in their play.

The moms and dads will note with wonder
Gary and Bernie's antique plunder;
The sturdiness of beams and floor,
The perfect taste of their décor.

While Gramps and Grandma content will be
To listen to music or watch TV,
And in their hearts to feel great thanks
That God has blessed their growing ranks.

We gained a son-in-law last year,
But Bo and Karen won't appear.
We'll miss them both, 'tis truth to say,
It's Karen's first Christmas to be away.

If Dottie comes in her Pontiac,
We'll sit by the fire and yakety-yak
And watch children in their glee
Longingly gaze at the Christmas tree.

With Bernie, the footman and Gary, the cook,
We'll play we're characters in a book
And call to mind that far off day
When this house sheltered Henry Clay.

And then of history we'll think
As we remember Congressman Finck.
But Underwood we'll not revere;
Begone, you sot, with *all* your beer.

The snapping and crackling of the Yuletide log
And the frisky capers of Amy, the dog,
Will mingle with carols old and sweet
To make a Christmas that's complete.

A vote of thanks we'll give our hosts
And drink to them the Wassail toast
And pray their house will a future cast
As glorious as its noble past.

By Isabelle Martin
(aka Mom)

   Little did we know that there were nests of black snakes in the basement of this beautiful old home. When we sold the house the following summer, the new owners had to have an exterminating company come and remove 150 black snakes. I would have died if I had known they were there at the same time we were. The heating system was hot water and the furnace was outside in a shed for safety. It pumped hot water heat through underground pipes into the house. We didn't have much need to go into the basement. I remember sanding flocked wallpaper off the dining room walls. It took two weeks! The previous owners, the Underwoods, must have used Crazy Glue to hang it. They also painted around furniture!

While we were there, we met the "Wallpaper Lady." She was heavy-set and could do a large room in a day with just a ladder, a broom, and some razor blades. She used to look up at the ceiling, examine the paper to be cut, look away, and then cut it. It was always perfect. She didn't charge much either if you kept beer in the refrigerator for her. She was a blessing!

We completed ten homes in ten years while we were together, and we made money on every one of them. I will share some of the more interesting memories about these homes.

One home we bought in Groveport, Ohio, was right in the downtown section of this small town. In one of the upstairs bedrooms, we noticed that the ceiling was starting to turn brown. Gary decided to take a look in the attic. He got a ladder, put a lamp in the opening, and stuck his head in. And then he screamed! I didn't know what to think. He said there were hundreds of bats hanging upside down, grinning at him! An exterminator removed them and filled several large garbage bags full of guano, otherwise known as bat poop! After Gary put it all on his garden for fertilizer, we found out that we could have sold each bag for quite a lot of money. The flowers sure bloomed beautifully that summer though!

Another memory about this home features Gary and me working until midnight to put up this very difficult wallpaper on one wall. I had taught school all day and we were both tired when we finished. Gary made each of us a cup of tea so we could relax and admire our work. Unfortunately the time for admiration didn't last very long; we had put the paper on upside down! We finished our tea and went to bed. We decided to fix the mistake the following day. This home is on the National Register of Historic Homes.

We started to collect antiques as a hobby at this time, and we went to auctions sometimes with just five dollars. We got better and more selective, and soon we could fill our antique homes with antique furniture.

Our favorite home was a Georgian brick colonial home in Royalton, Ohio. It was absolutely stunning, but it needed work on everything. I paid eighteen thousand dollars for it years ago and it sold recently for two hundred and sixty-seven thousand dollars! It was built in 1803, the same year that Ohio became a state, and was the oldest home we'd restored.

This home was heated by oil, and the first winter we were there, we had so much snow that the snow banks were as high as the power lines along the road where they had been plowed. There were times when the oil truck couldn't get to our home. So we burned wood. The home had a winding three-story stairway and five fireplaces, each designed by a master carpenter, John Leist, a cabinetmaker who built four homes in the area. You could stand upright in the fireplace in the kitchen. This home was also on the National Register of Historic Homes and is featured in the Fairfield Historic Society's book, *Architecture and Arts*. I hated to leave this home, but I will explain why I had to in a later chapter.

We purchased another large wooden home in Lancaster, Ohio. This is where my aunt crashed into three cars and broke her leg. This home didn't need as much work, and it was easier to restore. It had two rooms in the front, a parlor and a less formal living room. There were many fireplaces and two sets of stairs. We were happy that it had no bats or snakes! The yard was beautiful and had a stone fence that reached back to a three-car garage. There were two upstairs balconies and a screened in porch off the kitchen. The kitchen was my favorite room in the house.

The home was on the historic tour in Lancaster, and it was chosen by the *Columbus Dispatch* to be displayed in the newspaper. We had two full pages of coverage and over 200 guests. It was fun but tiring.

Chapter 7

TWO PLUS ONE MAKE THREE

WHEN I first got the job at Champion Middle School in Columbus, Ohio, it had an all-black student population, and I was one of only three white teachers. The building was built in the late 1800s and was badly in need of repairs. At one time, it was the only middle school that would hire black teachers.

The black principal called me into his office and said, "Mr. Martin, your resume looks good, but you're kind of small, and some of your students will be six feet tall. I think you might have a hard time making it here!" I'm 5' 3", and that's exaggerating a little, but I replied, "Just wait and see!" He laughed, liked my spirit, and supported me the entire year. I needed the job – I was broke. I put everything I had into my teaching and started to read every book I could find that was written by African-American authors.

This was right after Dr. Martin Luther King had been shot, and there was a lot of hostility and mistrust between the two races. I made sure my bulletin boards were African-American oriented. And I made sure that all my students knew that I was crazier than they were, so they'd better not mess with me! They liked that and responded positively. It was like being short but carrying a long stick. The students soon respected me and started competing with each other for the best grades.

At the end of my third year, I received the Teacher of the Year award, voted on by staff members. (See picture) I still prize this award! Only one teacher was difficult to work with while I was there – she actually encouraged my students to act out in my classes. I just figured she was a nut case. She came into my room after school just to check out my bulletin boards. The rest of the staff was very supportive, especially Mr. Byrd, a black math teacher. I treated him like my mentor, and he was very helpful, as he could see I was sincere. I received the Teacher of the Year award again a few years later.

Over the years, our student population changed because of desegregation laws. At first we had forced busing of white students to promote integration, but before they came, one million dollars were spent on improvements to the building. I remember that, because when it snowed, the snow piled up on the floor underneath the crack under the window. They replaced all of the windows.

Slowly, over time, even the bus population brought more and more black students rather than the intended white students to help desegregate the school. And soon it became a mostly all-black school again. It wasn't long before they stopped bussing altogether.

After teaching English to regular classes, I applied for the Title I Reading position at the same school building. My classes consisted of eight to ten students selected for the class because they had the lowest reading scores in the school. This was tougher than it sounds because with low reading scores came other problems—short attention spans, behavioral problems, and some downright meanness. I always tried to keep an open mind because I knew what their lives at home were like. For example, one student begged me all year to come to his home to meet his grandfather. I had a reading contest every year to challenge students to read books. Then I rewarded the winner with ten dollars. Well, one year, this particular student won and he begged me to meet his grandfather. So I stopped by his house, and his grandfather let me in. In the main room sat a group of men, all smoking weed. But even more discouraging were the blown-up nude pictures of the boy's mother in provocative positions hanging on the walls. They all acted as though nothing was out of the ordinary.

When the school's first principal transferred to a high school, he was replaced with one of the least supportive principals I've ever worked with. He praised no one and tried to make life miserable for all the teachers and staff. He had a bad temper and was a total control freak as well.

One day, he asked me if I would cover another teacher's class, as she had an import telephone call. When I walked into the room, a student had his desk held high over his head and was ready to lambast somebody over the head with it. His name was Robert Walker. I really didn't know him, but knew his name. I said quietly, "Robert, put the chair down." He was big and muscular. He replied, "Yes, sir," and put it down, and I thought I was a heavenly being. He could have badly injured the student or me!

Later I later asked him why he was going to throw his desk at another student and he said that this boy was making fun of the way he smelled. Well, Robert smelled like urine because he had to share a bed with his little brother, Boo, who wet the bed every night, and Robert's grandmother, the person who was in charge of the household, wouldn't let him take a bath in the morning. As soon as I could, I talked his grandmother into letting Robert take a morning bath instead of an evening one.

Next year Robert was in my class. I had visited his home a few times because I often visited students' homes. He lived with his aged grandmother, his older sister, whom I had taught earlier, and his little brother, Boo. His mother was a serious alcoholic, and his aunt was a serious heroin addict, and they didn't come around much unless there was something in it for them.

During this time, Gary and I were working on the Georgian colonial home. One day, the principal walked into my classroom, which Robert was in, and told me quietly that Robert's mother had been found dead. They didn't know if she had been murdered or not and little time was spent investigating. She was promiscuous and so Robert had never known who his father really was. The principal asked me if I would drive Robert home, and he said he would cover my class for me. I agreed and took Robert out into the hall to give him the awful news. He immediately took off running. The principal asked me to follow him in my car to make sure he got home safely.

I drove down the street, and there was Robert, holding a broken wine bottle, ready to kill the man he thought had beaten his mother to death. I pulled up beside him and quietly said, (well, it had worked once!) "Robert, put the bottle down and get into the car." He did exactly as I told him, and we rode silently to his grandmother's house.

When we got there, his grandmother was lying across the bed, weeping. When she saw Robert, she said that she was going to have to take him downtown. "Downtown" meant Child Protective Services. I thought for a moment and offered to take Robert home with me until after the funeral, and she agreed. I helped plan the funeral, as the grandmother had no idea what to do. I offered to take Robert to get a suit at Lazarus, which is now Macy's, and he asked me what I was willing to pay for it. I said, "I think you can get a sports jacket and some dress pants for around thirty dollars."

He said, "Wow! I can buy two suits for that at the department store in my neighborhood."

So, I gave him thirty dollars and waited in the car. He went in and came out with the cheapest, limpest, baby-blue suit I had ever seen, and he had change to spare!

After the funeral was over and the collection plate was passed around to buy liquor for later, I discovered that Robert had some bad memories of his mother. One time he told me that she would always come around at Christmas time, when his grandmother had saved money for presents, to ask if she could have the money. She always promised Robert that she would be back Christmas Day with his presents. She never came. Robert always got his presents from charities.

A day after the funeral, I was planning to drop Robert off at his grandmother's house. But instead, she asked me if I could keep him one more week. I agreed and said, "You'll probably be able to handle Robert in a week."

Wow, was I wrong! One week stretched into a month, and a month turned into two more. I realized that she didn't really want Robert back. And I couldn't bear to see Robert go downtown because I knew he was too old to be adopted. Gary and I didn't really mind because Robert was strong and could break up a sidewalk we no longer needed with a sledgehammer. Robert's grandmother kept Boo for as long as she could, then he went to Children's Services to live and hopefully to be adopted. When he wasn't adopted, he went to live in a group home. Robert's sister, Jesteen, was several years older, and she lived with her grandmother for awhile, and then went out on her own.

Robert soon started calling me "Dad," and I liked the sound of that. I helped him with his homework, and his grades improved. Then one day, we were sitting in a restaurant and eating lunch, and he asked me, "Dad, why don't you just adopt me?' I nearly fell off the lunch-counter stool! After I regained my composure, I said, "Let me think about it."

I pondered it over a few days, and I thought, *Why not?* But I knew I had to ask my lover first. Robert called him Mr. Gary, and they got along splendidly. It was fine with Gary, and he liked the idea and wished he could adopt Robert himself. That was easy!

The next part was asking his grandmother. When I did, she smiled and said with her somewhat Southern drawl, "Why aren't you the nicest." I didn't know if she really meant it or not. So I pushed further and said,

"I mean legally adopt him." She said she would think about it and tell me the next day.

The next day she agreed on the condition that Robert would come to see her every now and then and scrub her kitchen floor. I agreed to this condition. I let Robert drive on the country road that evening, even though he was underage. I had been giving him a few driving lessons. He was thrilled at the prospect of driving and even more thrilled at the prospect of being legally adopted. He drove home very carefully, and I reminded him that we weren't through with the adoption process yet.

Now I had to go to court. Because his grandmother had agreed, it was a fairly simple process. A social worker had to talk to Robert, his grandmother, and make two home visitations. Then she would make her recommendation. It took about two months, but she wrote a glowing report. As she shook my hand, she told me that I was the first white, single male to adopt a black child in the state of Ohio. Robert was thrilled, and so was I. He got a new birth certificate with just one parent on it—me! I would have been just seventeen years old and a senior in high school! I had actually planned to go to law school and become a lawyer at this time, but instead took on the responsibility of raising a young adult who was way behind academically. Best choice I ever made!

Robert became the new star in middle school. By then, there were several white teachers at my school, and all the teachers would send Robert up to me when he acted up in class, which he didn't do very often. There was one black teacher, Mrs. Welch, who was very strict and used the paddle often, as most of us did in those days. One day, she sent Robert up to me with a note. It read, "Robert rolled his eyes at me, and it was very disrespectful." I knew she was Robert's favorite teacher, but he also knew what she expected me to do. I took him out into the hall, paddled him twice, and sent him back in tears to apologize to her. He could indeed roll his eyes, and if they had been darts, you would be dead. I only had to paddle Robert one more time; again it was for rolling his eyes at me. This time he was much older and bigger than I was. He could have taken that paddle and broken it in half over my head. But instead his eyes watered up, and he apologized.

Robert was fairly easy to teach; it seemed as if he were just like a sponge and soaked everything up. He was still behind in reading, so I bought him several books by African-American authors. For every book he read and summarized it satisfactorily, I gave him a dollar. Sometimes, he woke me up late at night and said, "Hey, you owe me a dollar!" I knew the only way he could catch up to his grade level in reading was to read a lot, and it worked.

I thought Robert could go to high school in Amanda, Ohio, a few miles down the road from our house. I figured he would be okay in a country school because he was already getting to know some of the neighbors who lived across the street who would also attend the same high school. It was either that or ride into Columbus with me every morning and go to East High School. This was an all-black school with a poor academic record, and the two school's daily schedule didn't match.

But God works in mysterious ways and had a different plan. One day, Robert was cutting the grass with a riding mower and a car full of high-school students yelled out, "Nigger!" And I heard it! I thought, *no son of mine is going to a school where the students don't respect him.* Soon after, there was a "For Sale" sign in our front yard. The first people who came through agreed to our asking price, and a month later, we were living in the large Lancaster home that we had on tour. Robert was able to go to Lancaster High School, a beautiful new building with state of the art football facilities. And there were other African-American students there as well.

As an aside, my parents loved Robert, especially my dad. Robert and he ate popcorn and watched basketball games together, something my dad and I never did. Meanwhile, my mom and I played Scrabble in the kitchen. She usually beat me!

I had taught Robert how to drive by then so he could get a driver's license. I will never forget how he almost killed me by running a stop sign! I was driving a bright green 850 Fiat Sports Coupe with a black convertible top. I needed a new car, so I gave the Fiat to Robert. He shined it up beautifully, and it looked like new.

I learned that if Robert had a problem and wouldn't talk to me, I could always help him wash his car on Saturday, and he would open up to me. We had some of our best conversations shining that car.

I felt comfortable knowing he could drive home after football practice, and if I was not home yet, he could let himself into the house. Robert became the star running back on the football team; he even had O. J. Simpon's number "42" on his jersey. He was always polite, answering questions with "Yes, ma'am," or "No, sir," and everybody learned to like him. In fact, at his school's open house, one of the younger coaches came up to me and told me that if he ever had a son, he would like for him to be just like Robert. I thought that was the nicest compliment I was ever given.

Everybody liked him except for one: a white, opinionated, English teacher who wanted him to be tested for special education. They called my school to get my permission to test him. I said, "Hold on. I'll be right there!"

I got in my car and flew down to Lancaster. I demanded a conference with the teacher and principal and gave them, especially the teacher, an earful. Basically I said, "Robbie (that's what everyone called him) is a unique child—he has suffered a great deal in his short lifetime. I had him in my class in middle school, and he does not belong in a special education class. If he does not measure up to your expectations, then it's your responsibility to motivate him to meet your expectations. In fact, that's what the state is paying you to do. I will work with you, if you will work with Robert. And I will **not** give my permission for him to be tested."

I got up, thanked them, and left. This English teacher was one of the worst teachers I've ever had the "pleasure" of meeting. She assigned a list of twenty-five difficult and esoteric spelling words a week that you wouldn't use in your whole lifetime! The students were responsible for memorizing their definitions and for spelling them correctly. I worked every evening on those stupid words with him, but Robert finally got the hang of it and got a C for the year. I heaved a sigh of relief! Several times during his last two years, Robert made the Honor Roll.

I was pretty hard on Robert. One time the head football coach called me about Robert's grades, which were slipping during football season, and I said he couldn't play football in the upcoming game and had to sit on the bench. Robert was angry with me. The coach thought I was being a little rough on him, but Robert's grades never dipped during football season after that.

Because he was an outstanding football player, a large picture of Robert hung in the town's only downtown department store. Every business featured one of the football players, but Robert's picture was right downtown where everybody could see it! Lancaster was a football town. It shut down on Friday nights, and everybody turned out for the big game. Two of our lesbian friends would come down from Columbus every Friday night to go with Gary and me to every one of Robert's games. The lesbians taught me all the rules of the game so I could understand what was going on! We sat in the parents' section in the bleachers, and it was exciting when Robert ran down the field and all the parents shouted, "Go,

Robbie!" Then they would turn to us and give us the thumbs up. Robert always looked up to see if we were there before each game. Robert moved slowly when he wasn't on the field, but he could run like a deer when he had the football.

We had a very tiny, miniature, black and white mutt with the cutest face I have ever seen on a dog. Her name was Abigail, but we called her Abby for short. Abby loved Robert. At night she couldn't make up her mind if she wanted to stay up with me or go to bed with Robert. She usually ended up in bed with Robert. She would" scoot" under the covers until she reached the bottom of the bed, turn around three times, and then let out a big sigh. Then, when I would go to bed, she would "scoot" her way back up under the covers and come running into my room and repeat the process all over in my bed. She would stay at the bottom of my bed, next to my feet, for about fifteen minutes, and then "scoot" back up and run back to Robert's room and start all over again. She would keep this up for about an hour before she finally made up her mind who she wanted to sleep with. Sometimes it would be me, and other times it would be Robert. She is part of my wonderful memories, and I loved that dog!

But not everything was hunky-dory for Robert. I remember one time I was late getting home; it was cold, and Robert had lost his key. He was curled up in the fetal position, shivering. I felt like a failure as a father, but we found a place to hide a key, and all ended well.

Another time, Robert asked me if I would drive a couple of his football buddies home after football practices. On the drive, Robert said something grammatically incorrect, and they all laughed at him. He didn't say anything, but I could tell by the look on his face that he was hurt. Actually, this experience made it easier for me to correct his grammar because he didn't want to be laughed at again.

One time we stopped to see his grandmother, who always had a pie to sell me for ten dollars She listened to Robert speak for awhile, and then she said, "Boy, why you gittin' so uppity? You didn't use to speak like that." I always bought the pie even though I could see cockroaches crawling all around her oven.

On the way home, I explained to Robert what "bidialectism" meant and told him it would be all right for him to talk one way to his grandmother and another way when he might be interviewing for a job. He understood, and to this day he can "get down" with certain people and speak grammatically correct English with others.

I met Jim Saunders in Lancaster, a black man about my age, and he shared with me the history of the close ties shared by the fifteen or so black families in Lancaster. Robert's best friend was a member of one of these families and in the same grade. But the interesting part was that Jim's father was Robert's grandmother's brother! All the black families in Lancaster were distantly related to each other in some way. That meant that Robert couldn't date any of the black girls because they were all cousins of some kind or another. What Jim told me was that the black Poindexter families had migrated from southern Ohio to Columbus years ago. But some got stuck along the way and settled in other cities. They all protected and supported each other in Lancaster.

This indirectly caused a problem for Robert on prom night. This white girl from a wealthy family had taken a liking to Robert, and so he asked her to go to the prom with him. She said, "Yes," and a few days before he rented a tuxedo and ordered her a corsage. But a day before the prom, she called and cancelled—another heartbreak. But he was resilient and recovered quickly.

I recall another incident along the same line; Robert and I were eating in a favorite restaurant "Roots" in Lancaster and we were sitting by a table with two older couples. We ordered our food, and then they started talking very loudly about "Negroes were moving into white communities and lowering the home values etc." They were saying it loud enough so that Robert couldn't help but hear. I sat still until I couldn't take it anymore. I started to get up to give them a piece of my mind. Robert just reached over and grabbed my shoulders and sat me back down. He said, "You're not used to hearing things said like this; I've heard them all my life. You can't go around trying to fix everything." I learned patience and to pick and choose the battles that I wished to fight.

Chapter 8
THE PROBLEM FOR ME

E VERY child, and adult for that matter, desires and needs acceptance from his or her parents. For me, with my mother's beliefs, it was very difficult to feel unconditionally accepted or loved when one part of me was rejected. I think one's sexuality is a big part of anyone's being, and especially for a child or a young adult, this part can't be negated. I loved my mother and still do. But her way of interpreting the Bible, and even going beyond the Bible, with her idea of sanctification—which isn't even mentioned in the Bible—had personal consequences for me.

Once my parents learned I was gay, their whole mission became to change me into a heterosexual so I could go to Heaven. Soon the whole family heard I was gay. I remember when my brother found out, his wife jumped out of the car and asked, "Is it contagious or hereditary? Can our children become gay too?"

I was there at the time; she said this in front of me. I was very young and had no argument for her. They changed their feelings and attitudes toward me as time went on. My brother could only talk about cars with me; for years, I drove a Mercedes Benz and later a Lexus. That's all we conversed about. I soon realized, at family gatherings, my opinion no longer counted for much, especially when my older brother and my dad talked about politics. I used to join in and was an accepted conversationalist. Not anymore.

This was at the time of the beginning of the AIDS epidemic. I noticed that my mom boiled my silverware; I think she did it at the suggestion of my brother, but I'm not sure. We would always get together at my parents' home for all of the holidays, but I noticed some of the family started not showing up.

I also remember the time when I sensed that some of my brothers and sisters did not want me to be around their older male children. These were my nephews, and I loved them, and I wasn't a pedophile!

Christmas was always a big event in our household. I went home every Christmas and took Robert and Gary with me. Mom loved to buy presents, and she bought them even when they couldn't afford to. Gary was always generous and bought my mom lovely gifts. Sometimes, when he worked at a florist shop, he brought her a beautiful flower arrangement. But year after year, Robert and I would get nice presents, but Gary would inevitably get one pair of socks or something else of little significance. All the other in-laws received thoughtful and sometimes expensive presents. This always hurt my feelings.

I also remember when Gary and I split up – we had been together ten years – and I went to my parent's home to clear my head. My younger sister divorced her husband of three years and we both ended up at home on the same weekend. My family cared for her, prayed with her, let her cry on their shoulders, while I sat outside on the edge of the front porch and could say nothing about my splitting up with Gary. When I left to go back to Columbus, I said out loud to myself, "Bernie, you no longer have a family here." I was also hurt and needed their love and understanding. My younger sister, Karen, the psychiatric nurse, was generally a little more understanding, but this time she absolutely ignored me.

But the biggest problem was when I spent time alone with my mother. She always made graham cracker pudding for me—my favorite dessert. After everyone left (I was the only one who stayed overnight, because I was from out of state), and all the others had gone home or to bed, Mom would ask me to play Scrabble with her and enjoy some of her delicious graham cracker pudding. We always played on the kitchen table. We talked about my teaching and other things of interest to her, but it always ended with the same question. "Have you decided to become straight so you can get into heaven?" When my father came in and heard what we were talking about, he would excuse himself and go to bed. Later, I understood why.

Sometimes, our conversations were amiable; other times she got almost nasty, and then she let me know, in no uncertain terms, that the direction I was going in would land me straight in hell.

I always asked her if she thought she could get Dad or my brothers or brothers-in-law to try to become gay. I told her I was born this way. I told her I knew at the age of six that there was something different about me. I asked her, "Why would I choose to become gay and have to take all the harassment growing up or listen to all the gay jokes in the teachers' lounge without being able to respond in any way? Why would I become gay if it meant I couldn't get my lover's name on my mortgage without any luck?"

She listened, but she wouldn't budge. I don't know why I needed her to be on my side, but I did. I later believed that I never really felt completely loved by her because she couldn't tolerate a big part of who I was. And she succeeded in making me feel guilty at times. My brothers and sisters always thought my mom catered to me and spent more time with me than with the others. I think that was because I was a good student and reader and could discuss *Moby Dick* with her when I was only eight years old.

We spent every holiday with my family, and I always went to Elkhart, Indiana, when school closed for the summer and again before school started in the fall. Each time was the same routine. It got so that I armed myself with ammunition to persuade her to change her mind.

One time I told her that I knew from my studies that the Bible had been translated repeatedly, and different interpretations were written that spoke to different cultures. I explained the various names for God— Jehovah, Yahweh, and Adonai (translated from Hebrew, it means God). The New Jerusalem Bible used Elohim, the Alpha and Omega, Lord, the Almighty, Root of David, Lion of the Tribe of Judah, Messiah, King of Kings and Lord of Lords. I also expressed to her that there was no Hebrew word that connected with the connotation of same-sex relationships. The story of Sodom, which so many Christian anti-gay people use, really meant that the people of Sodom were not hospitable. When the angels asked Lot to send them their male visitors, they wished to bargain with them. That's why his virgin daughters were finally offered. It was considered a sin not to be hospitable. How Sodom and Gomorrah came to be associated with same-gender sex is through all the various translations of the story and particularly the differences in the meaning of the word "Yada." Sodom was judged to be sinful and was condemned to be destroyed because God could not find even ten righteous people in the city. If you look up Sodom and Gomorrah on the internet, you will find many versions of the same story, coming from the many interpretations of the Bible. But I believe that my God does not discriminate, and my interpretation of the story does not involve same-gender sex.

I also used the argument that many Christian anti-gay people used specific verses in the Bible to cast same-sex relationships as immoral and un-Christian. But they ignored other scriptures such as, for example, that it was a sin to wear clothing made from two different kinds of material.

I explained to her that some Christians believed that being gay was a choice made by individuals, and I had hoped that she would understand that my own life story did not substantiate this idea. I told her that groups of people who were opposed to same-sex lifestyles would use the Bible to endorse their rejection while at the same time using the Bible to support heterosexual relationships. Jesus himself was mute on the subject of homosexuality and, in fact, there was no such word in the Hebrew language for "homosexuality." In Leviticus, codes were given to the Jews to set them apart from other nations; Christians uphold some of these codes in their anti-gay argument but ignore other codes altogether. Even Paul's letters to the various churches claim that "idolatry" is the most severe sin.

I tried to get my Mom to read some of the literature put out by the Parents, Families, and Friends of Lesbians and Gays (PFLAG). She thought it was just propaganda and wouldn't even try to change her way of thinking. She never mentioned the Stonewall Union's uprising in New York City, as if it didn't exist. She never talked about all the gays who were dying of AIDS or committing suicide because of harassment or because of growing up in households that rejected them.

After I did all my homework, read all of my books, and gave her all of my arguments, she still wouldn't budge. In fact, she suffered from Alzheimer's disease and, after going through every single stage of the disease, she still held to her belief that I was going straight to hell until she no longer recognized me. She died at age 94 of Alzheimer's. I loved my mother; I even went to up to the nursing home a few times and fed my mom. She introduced me to her friends as her husband. For these visits, I left Columbus at five in the morning, got to the nursing home in time for lunch, fed my mother, and drove back to Columbus in the evening.

I also knew how much my mother liked to buy us all Christmas presents, even though eventually my parents could no longer afford to do so. It was then that I would slip my dad a check for five hundred dollars, and he wouldn't say a word to anyone. I wanted it that way.

Finally, in desperation, I told my mother that I was a Christian and was going to heaven. Neither she nor anyone else could deter me from this belief. She let up on me a little bit after that, but she still argued with me that I was going to go to hell unless I became heterosexual.

Believing that there is a superior being to mankind is easy for me. When I was young, I just took it on faith. I prayed, but not in the way my mother did. I talked to God as if He was my personal friend, while driving in the car, or doing whatever I was doing. I would turn to Him in times of trouble and felt that He listened and answered many of my prayers.

In later years, after watching shows such as *NOVA* and *Animal Planet* about the intricacies of nature and the complicated inner workings of many different species, I felt I had no choice but to believe. And as for the questions I had had as a child, I read enough from the Bible to understand that my sins were already covered by the grace of God through his Son, who died on the cross for mankind's sins.

John 3, verse 16 says, "For God so loved the world that he gave his only begotten Son, that whosoever believeth in him should not perish, but have everlasting life." In my view, "whosever" doesn't have any strings attached—it isn't limited to anyone based on gender, race, age, or sexuality. Those are God's own words.

I also know that we are all made in God's image. Any problem I originally had with million-year-old bones of prehistoric skeletons that I couldn't fit into the King James Bible's time framework, I no longer had to. I decided that I did not need to understand everything. I haven't been around for a million years, so some questions have to be left unanswered. And, I'm okay with that.

I have a rather simplistic view of Heaven and God's plan for us. I know God is the Alpha and Omega. When I look at the wonderful things right here on earth that God has created, such as hearing a choir sing in St. Patrick's Cathedral in New York City—which was made by man—I realize how much greater Heaven will be. I believe in grace, and I know that I must have faith in order to believe or accept the things I do not understand. I figure that if God wanted us to know everything, there would be no need for faith. My mortal mind can't even wrap itself around how much greater than earth His Heaven will be. And this excites me, fills me with anticipation, and makes me eager to find out what Heaven will be like. I don't have to fill in all the gaps. I know I have to obey the Ten Commandments and try to live the most honest life I can. But beyond that, there is nothing else I can do to get into heaven; the price has already been paid through the blood of Jesus. I know I will make mistakes or sin in thoughts, words, and deeds because I am human. As Shakespeare put it, "To err is to be human." I do not know God's plan—I don't know what his time frame is. A day may be a single year or a million years. I just know that he is preparing us a place in Heaven that will be better than anything we can imagine on earth. Isn't that a wonderful thought? I know my mother and I never reached an agreement, and it caused me much pain throughout my life, but I know I will see her in heaven, and maybe we can sort it all out then.

I believe the best term for my kind of religion is a Christian with deep spiritual beliefs. I believe in helping mankind and have tried to do this all my life—in my professional teaching career and in my own personal life. I remember at my mother's funeral, my Uncle Al, a Baptist, put his arm around me and said, "Bernie, just know that I love you even when you don't know about other members of your family." He said no more, but I understood immediately what he was talking about, and it meant the world to me. When my mother stopped recognizing who I was, I felt sad; I knew then we would never come to any kind of agreement. I think my mother's idea of sanctification made her very unhappy. It was impossible for her, or for any person really, to live without making mistakes or transgressing in thought, word, and deed. She never seemed genuinely happy, and that made me sad.

We were a close-knit family, but my parents did teach us to be independent, so as we got older, many of us went our separate ways with children, careers, etc.

Chapter 9
LATER LIFE AND CAREER

WHEN Robert graduated from high school, he got a full scholarship to play football at Muskingum College in Ohio. He matriculated with his friend, and they roomed together. Robert had been the first one in his family to graduate from high school, and he was excited to go to college. The coach assured me that they would give Robert all the academic help he needed.

During his first football game, he broke his leg and was told he would be out for the rest of the season. By this time, his roommate had already left to return home—homesickness, no doubt! One night I got a call from Robert, and he asked, "Dad, can I please come back home?"

I realized Robert wasn't ready to leave home yet either. And it became clear that he would not receive any academic help because he could no longer play football. I think he felt ashamed, as if he had let me down. I didn't feel that way and welcomed him back home. He then joined the Air Force but was released early when they discovered he had flat feet. Robert was kind of lost for a while.

During the year leading up to Robert's freshman year in college, Gary started to change. I think he was tired of restoring historic homes, and I think he became envious of the amount of time I spent with Robert, tutoring him every evening. I think he felt like a third wheel.

One night I got a call from someone I didn't know who claimed he was having sex with Gary. I didn't know what to make of it—was it true or just a hoax? I confronted Gary; he admitted it was true, and he moved in with this man. Their relationship lasted a few weeks, and then Gary went his own way.

After ten years of being in this relationship, my heart was broken. Gary and I shared so many memories, and I knew that Robert was leaving for college in less than a year. Gary never tried to come back just then, and I'm not sure how I would have reacted if he had. He just started to float from place to place after that. He started going to the gay bar in Newark, Ohio, and eventually he moved in with some of our mutual straight friends.

This was a low point in my life. I wasn't going to leave Robert hanging academically, so I couldn't devote more time to Gary, and I wasn't sure that I would have anyway after he had been unfaithful.

I sold the Lancaster home and rented a home in town. I felt like we all spent the next year in limbo. I hadn't been to a gay bar as a single person for ten years, and I was a little overwhelmed at even the thought of starting over. It was no easier for Robert; by this time he really liked Gary and missed him a great deal. I came out to Robert a few months before, and basically all he said was, "I already knew." I guess some things you just can't hide. Robert tried to find work and bounced from job to job.

By this time the Fiat was in fairly bad condition. Robert was working in a fast food restaurant, Taco Bell, I think, and traded the Fiat for a small, light-blue truck that seemed to me to be held together with paper clips and rubber bands.

When I finally got the nerve to start going back to gay bars, I was initially very uncomfortable. But I am not one who likes to live alone. I like to have someone to love and share things with.

One night as I was leaving a bar, I turned around and saw a good-looking black man just entering. Something told me to turn around and go back in. This is when I met Jessie, and we became instant lovers. We stayed together for the next twenty-two years. Jessie moved in with Robert and me, and he worked for Anchor Hocking, a large company which sold kitchenware, until the company moved out of state. When Anchor Hocking closed for good, it had a devastating effect on the town of Lancaster. Second and third generations of families had dedicated their careers to Anchor Hocking, and a strong union guaranteed good wages. It took years for Lancaster to fully recover.

I grew tired of renting and bought two houses side by side in Bexley. I figured we could rent out one, live in the other, remodel the first one, sell it, move into the second house, remodel it, and sell that one too. I figured we'd make pretty good money. However, Jessie didn't have the knowledge for restoration that Gary had, and I ended up doing most of the work or teaching him to help me.

One day before we left Lancaster, I was lying on the couch when Gary walked in, apologetic and ready to resume our relationship. I had been with Jessie a few months and felt myself caught up in a bind. When I told Gary I was already in another relationship, he was very disappointed and left. Again, he was in limbo.

After Robert came back from the military, he shortly moved in with his girlfriend, who was white. I never cared that much for her, as she took way too long to introduce him to her parents. I felt as if she might be rebelling against her parents and was using Robert to do it. I didn't say too much; I knew Robert had to work things out for himself. I did visit them at their apartment, and when I opened the refrigerator door, I found there was no food in it. I talked to Robert, assuring him he was still my son and letting him know that before he ever went hungry he should call me and I would help him financially. That's what parents do.

At this point, I felt I had taken on more than I could chew. I was feeling like a failure as a father. I had really wanted Robert to graduate from college. I did, however, have the memory of Robert's grandmother's face light up with pride as he was handed his high school diploma. For me, that would have to suffice for a while.

With Robert gone and not much needing to be done to my home, I started to seriously try to advance my career. After Jessie got his general equivalency diploma (GED), he attended Ohio State University (OSU) but had a difficult time. He transferred to Ohio Dominican College, a smaller Catholic college, where he could receive more individualized help from the nuns.

I started on my master's degree in Curriculum and Supervision at OSU. I just wanted to get it over with so I could get my pay increase and get on with my life. I decided to take as many classes as possible; I started one summer and finished at the end of the next, without taking any breaks from teaching. I graduated with all A's and one B+.

The second summer, I took five classes, which was the maximum amount you could take. I ended up with three final exams on a Thursday and two more the following Friday. One professor, whom I really liked and learned so much from, looked at me after my third exam and said I looked tired and worn out. I told him why, and he exclaimed, "Didn't you know that you could have spaced these exams out over several days?" I didn't know; nobody had told me, and I didn't ask. It actually felt kind of good to be in the classroom and learning again instead of teaching.

The hardest part was my final written exam, which I had opted for instead of an oral one. I studied and studied for this four-hour exam. I went to Wendy's and drank coffee and studied one area; then I went to McDonald's and drank coffee and studied for another area, etc. When I took the exam, I wrote, nonstop, for four hours. When I was finished, I was exhausted and in a daze. I have no idea how I got home.

By this time, we had bought and moved into another home in south Bexley, a beautiful stone cottage. When I got home from the exam, I was sitting in my car in front of my house, hunched over the steering wheel in a coma-like state, and I didn't know where I was, nor did I care! A week or so later my professor called me into his office and said he would like to sponsor me for a doctorate degree. I thanked him, got the hell out of there, and didn't return to OSU until I had cancer twenty-five years later.

One day, my controlling principal made Mr. Byrd cry in the hallway. You remember Mr. Byrd, my chosen mentor? He was a strong teacher, had the respect of the students and the community, and I couldn't bear to see what I saw.

By then, I was the Building Representative to our local teachers' union. Morale was really low among the teachers at my school, so I made an appointment with the president of the Columbus Education Association (CEA). I explained what it was like teaching under this unprofessional principal, and he agreed to have a meeting in the CEA building. For a moment, I wasn't sure anyone would come, out of fear of retaliation. But in the end, almost every teacher showed up and aired his or her grievances. The principal was transferred the following year to a place where he lasted one year, and when that school was about to file a grievance, he finally retired!

Then good things really started to happen for me and the other teachers. You had to be a good teacher to survive at our school, but we didn't have the perspective to help us see that. The next principal was one of the most polite persons I had ever known, both as an administrator and in his personal life. He taught us all to be better teachers by setting an example. He gave praise where it was due, and helped us to promote ourselves.

Soon, one teacher left to become an assistant principal of a large high school and another left to be the coordinator of a program. I was asked to take a written test to be in the second wave of outstanding teachers to be in the Peer Assistance and Review Program (PAR). This was a fairly new program for Columbus, consisting of about twenty good teachers who mentored between fifteen to eighteen new teachers and worked with three or four struggling teachers. My personality was fairly laid back, so I was given some of the most difficult struggling teachers. We visited the classrooms unannounced, wrote our observations, set goals, and monitored progress. The teachers were monitored for one year, and then we made recommendations as to whether or not they should be kept teaching in the system to a PAR Panel.

I had two very difficult cases in my three years in PAR. The first teacher could be described as "missing half of a sandwich to complete a full picnic basket." He didn't know his subject matter, and he was way too friendly with the female students. I read his record in the downtown office and discovered he was let go by another district without explanation. I reported this to the PAR Panel, and sure enough, abuse charges were filed against him before the year ended.

The other difficult case was dealing with a shop teacher. Actually, he was a very pleasant person, but he hadn't kept up-to-date with strategies on how to manage a classroom of difficult students. Old methods on new students don't work. I felt his class was unsafe because of the electrical saws and other equipment. He was always complaining about how badly the students behaved. I knew he had to go, but he was only one year from retirement. It was my responsibility to tell him he was not going to be getting a contract the following year. I was a little afraid of how he might react. He was little and wiry. I could imagine him jumping over a table and hitting me over the head with one of his hammers!

This is one of those times when I "lifted mine eyes unto the hills ..." and prayed. The PAR Panel offered me some protection. I refused. When I told him he would be fired, he did practically jump over a table, but he hugged me instead and said, "Finally, somebody is being honest with me." I just about dropped my teeth! I convinced CEA to use his many sick leave days in lieu of another year of teaching, and he retired with full pay.

The PAR Program really opened my eyes to the inner workings of a large city school system. In my three years in the program, I learned more about teaching than at any other time. I saw the good, the bad, and the ugly. I was lucky to have some wonderful teachers to work with, and to this day, I will always be supportive of teachers. I saw new teachers, who barely made enough to pay rent, buy supplies or clothing for poor students out of their own pockets. I saw them take home hours of work for which they received no extra pay. I also was a liaison professor for Ohio State

University and had around six student teachers. I had one who could have mentored me because she was that good! I had time to reflect on my own teaching methods.

Sometimes, the principals were more difficult to work with than the students were. In one school, an ex-military principal ruled by intimidation. I had to get along with him! He would walk right by me in the hallway; I would speak to him, he would just hold his head high and pretend he didn't see me. One day I needed to talk to him; he made me wait in the office while he messed around with some papers on his desk. He finally called me in, and said abruptly, "Come in, close the door, and sit down!" I decided to get things straight right from the get go. So I replied, "If you want the door closed you will have to close it, and if I want to sit down I will or if I want to stand up I will." He left me alone for the rest of the year!

At the end of the year, he asked to see my evaluations of the seven teachers I had in his building even though he wasn't supposed to. These were some of the best teachers I had in my three years in the PAR Program, and my evaluations reflected that. When he gave me his evaluations, they were almost word for word taken from mine. Six of the teachers requested a transfer with my blessing. He asked me why, and I told him, "Maybe if you had treated them better, they might have stayed"

The PAR Program lasted only three years, and then we were to go back into the classroom or elsewhere. But I learned more through in-service and watching various teaching styles than I had ever learned from a textbook.

That following summer, I was unemployed, but I tried to get back my old job at my former school. They chose someone else. I was devastated! I called down to the personnel office, and they had nothing available.

I was beginning to feel desperate until I got a call from a gentleman who was head of all the Title I curriculum areas in Columbus City Schools; he asked me if I would be interested in the Title I Reading Program Coordinator position for all of the seventeen middle schools in Columbus. That was one of the best calls I received in my life. Once again, I "lifted mine eyes unto the hills …," this time to give thanks.

But I only had a few weeks to prepare for the two-week in-service program for all the middle school Title I Reading teachers. There were two to five teachers in each building. That's when I met Mara, the other middle school coordinator. Mara has to be one of the smartest people I have ever met. She actually thinks on her feet as she presents a workshop; this was something I had to learn to do. We hit it off immediately. We both love to talk, and sometimes when we went for lunch, we would start talking, and then forget what we were doing or where we were going. She also has a great sense of humor. I learned a lot from her.

I also met Pat, the writing coordinator for the system, and Nancy, the elementary reading coordinator. We made a pretty good team! Except for Pat, we all worked out of the same office and got to know each other pretty well.

This was at a time when African-American writers such as Mildred Taylor, Beverley Naidoo, Walter Dean Meyers, and others began writing books for middle school students. There were others, like Gary Paulsen who wrote *Nightjohn,* a great book for teaching students to <u>want</u> to learn to read.

I'm not sure how I made it through those first two weeks, but I soon learned that I had some of the smartest, hardest-working Title I teachers to work with. Most had their master's degrees. They were receptive to my ideas, and I enjoyed coordinating their programs. I also had two of the nicest bosses one could have. One was Ernie, who was my direct boss, and he patiently taught me everything I know about computers. Ernie was African-American and knew about my adopting Robert as did all the teachers, and I think I was rewarded by his helpfulness. He never complained, always complimented, and was just a real gentleman. My other boss, Jim, had given me the job. I didn't have a lot of interaction with him, but he was very professional and had high expectations of the people who reported to him. His wife, Hope, also worked out of our office as an Elementary Reading Coordinator.

Three things helped me in this job that lasted the four years until I retired. The first was my own experience in the classroom. The second was my adoption of my son, Robert. Columbus was basically an African-American student school district with a few sections of the city which were Appalachian. The third thing was the time I spent in the PAR Program. Plus, one summer I read over twenty middle school novels.

I think one of my major contributions was teaching teachers to find books that students wanted to read. Most people like reading about others who are like themselves. There were very few African-American books when I was in the classroom and even fewer books oriented to Appalachian students. But that all had changed by the time I was chosen to be the Title I Coordinator. We had book fairs full of African-American and Appalachian books. Soon we got into other areas such as peace, sibling rivalry, alcoholism, different families and lifestyles, death and dying, harassment, school tensions and challenges, etc. Each teacher had a certain amount of federal dollars to spend, and because they had between eight and ten students per class, they could buy sets of books to read together.

We also had summer writing workshops where teachers were paid to write curriculum guides, and I let them choose which books to write guides for. They picked students' favorites. Interestingly, these were the same books that I paid Robert $1 each for reading. The guides were professionally done. The summer writing teams were enjoyable, and soon many of my teachers were planning the two-week in-service training they received before school started.

When the regular classroom teachers saw the books and study guides, they wanted them also. Somehow we scrounged enough from a grant to get the money needed to get study guides for each school and a corresponding set of books. For middle school students who know how to read but just don't like to, the best way to teach them and raise their scores is to get them to read more. Finding books they can relate to is the best way to do this.

I taught my teachers to practice action research, which is a way of thinking about how you are teaching instead of blaming students for failures. I did some research myself. I walked into a wonderful, black, female teacher's class, Michelle, and selected several books whose front covers depicted exactly what they were about. Then I asked the students to study the books' covers and pick out the one they would most likely read. The black students chose black-oriented books, and the white students chose the white-oriented books. I used this to show some teachers who were a little bit stubborn and still wanted to use the same old, dull books that didn't appeal to students or bring them success.

One of the things I was proudest of was the Title I Summer School Program we developed with a special federal grant. The program was called "Learning on the Go." Only forty students could attend, and enrollment was on a first-come, first-served basis. Parents or a custodian had to come the first night and sign for all the field trips the students were going to go on. Each class had four teachers. The students were given disposable cameras and could take a certain number of pictures per week for each week of school. Their pictures were developed each week, and they made scrapbooks and wrote about their pictures and why they took those particular shots. Most importantly perhaps, they read books that accompanied each field trip.

For example, they read a book about Holocaust survivors. Then we took them to a traditional German restaurant, Schmidt's, and they listened to a Holocaust concentration camp survivor's story. She showed them the serial number tattooed on her arm. The students asked many questions. Some of the students had never eaten in a restaurant before.

Another place we took them was to the Adena Mansion and garden tour. One day, they took a walking tour to our wonderful Columbus Public Library, and they each got their own library card. Another field trip included the outdoor theater production of *Tecumseh* in Chillicothe, Ohio. After the show, the students were allowed to meet with the actors.

The final trip was on a large bus up to Cleveland to see a Cleveland Indians baseball game and stop at the Cleveland Metro Rain Forest. This was a real "trip," literally! The air conditioning on the bus broke down, and we couldn't open any of the windows. There were forty middle school students with raging hormones and six super teachers. By the time we got to Cleveland, everyone was wet, and the teachers practically fell out of the bus. They earned every penny they got for this trip. And to make matters worse (for me), at the baseball game a student leaned over and threw up on my shoes—too much excitement, I think! This was a trip that made history, and I have great admiration for those teachers who survived. (I got our money back from the bus company!) We also stayed in a motel with a swimming pool. At night, we told the students that they could not leave their room once lights were out and that we would tape each door shut so that we would know if any student broke the rule. I think the adults were all too tired to use any tape – but the students didn't know!

This program was expensive, but teachers followed the students' progress the next school year, and their test scores rose significantly. Programs like this cost some money, but they do work. We had two years of this program, and then it was back to teaching to the state standardized tests.

Some of the authors that we used were: Walter Dean Meyers (we had him come speak to our students and teachers during the school year), Mildred Taylor, Roald Dahl, Mildred Pitts, Gary Paulson, Jerry Spinelli, Beverly Cleary, Virginia Hamilton, Patti Stern, and others. Some of the students in one class wrote to an author and she wrote a lengthy letter back to them. Students were really excited to receive a letter from an author of one of the books they had read – an excellent teacher!

In my opinion, America needs to wake up and understand that we need to pay for the success of future generations of students and give teachers time to teach values as well as subject matter. Values last a lifetime, while memorized facts typically don't. On the last night of the school program, parents were invited, and students had a chance to share their scrapbooks. They were very proud of their achievements!

One funny anecdote that happened while I was working as a reading coordinator was when my son stopped by to take me out to lunch. Years before, he had come home with an earring in his ear. I went off, saying, "How could you do such a thing? Nobody will ever hire you!" You get the picture. The next day the earring was gone, and it never came back. Then when it became really popular to wear one, I got a tiny stud. I wasn't sure whether Robert would notice it or not. We ate lunch, and he didn't say anything. When we got back to where I worked, he dropped me off, and as I got out of the car, he said, "And by the way, take that damn earring out!" We both just laughed.

All in all, I had a wonderful experience as a reading coordinator with the help of a lot of professionals, and no one will ever hear me complain about America's teachers. After thirty years in the field, I was tired and ready to retire!

Chapter 10

OH NO, NOT CANCER!

I'VE got to write this chapter about my cancer because it is the reason I had the time to write this book in the first place.

First of all, there are thirty people on my maternal side of the family—siblings, aunts, uncles, cousins—who have had cancer in one form or another. I'm in a trial study at the James Cancer Clinic at OSU because of this; they are studying the relationship between heredity and cancer. Many in my family, young and old, have died of the disease. Four people have it and are fighting it now.

Others, like my Aunt Lil, had it in their twenties. But, Aunt Lil said she was *not* having cancer in her body; so she starved herself, prayed every day, and drank hot water with enough broth to keep her alive for six months. And when she returned to the hospital, skinny as a rail, they found no trace of cancer in her body! She lived cancer-free until the age of 106.

My mother had both breasts removed when I was a sophomore in college. My younger sister, Karen, had breast cancer, and it metastasized in her brain, and she died on the day she would have received her first retirement check. My oldest brother, Glenn, had cancer somewhere else too, and it metastasized in his brain. He died before his book was published. My grandmother died from stomach cancer. The relatives in California died from melanoma.

As we were leaving the graveyard in Indiana, where one of my siblings was buried, the remaining siblings looked at each other and someone said, "I wonder which one of us will be next?" Little did I know it would be me.

Most of the rest of this will be humorous because cancer is ugly enough. For me to survive five years with malignant squamous cell carcinoma is a miracle, and I believe it is due, in part, to my sense of humor. But I will tell you just a few details, and then I will tell you the funny stories. Well, I hope they're funny to you because they are to me anyway!

It started as a pea-sized bump by the right side of my nose. It hurt! My family doctor, I think, got tired of listening to me complain about it and sent me to a neurologist. (Some doctors run fairly low on my list of people to praise, just above attorneys!) I think my family doctor thought I was a hypochondriac. The neurologist decided that I had trigeminal neuralgia—words I'd never heard of before and couldn't even pronounce—even though I had written my family history on the admittance form full of case after case of my family's cancer. He explained what trigeminal neuralgia was and convinced me because it matched all of my symptoms. Back then, just five years ago in 2007, there wasn't much they could do to fight this disease, but they could give you what I call "head meds." He must have given me nine or so head meds: Trileptal, Cerefolin, Amitriplyline, Gabapentin, Carbamazepine, Naproxen, etc. I was allergic to most of them, and the ones I was allergic to the most made me paranoid and schizophrenic. Most importantly, none of them helped me. This went on for eight months, and my little bump grew larger and larger. I would have episodes where the pain was so intolerable that I couldn't sit in a chair without sliding out of it onto the floor. I should have gone to another doctor for a second opinion, but, in my family, we grew up trusting the word of doctors.

I kept asking (after I went to the emergency room twice because of the pain), "Why don't you take a biopsy of this, particularly because my brother and sister so recently died from cancer?" The neurologist continued to insist I had trigeminal neuralgia (TN). I bought the bible on TN and read it from cover to cover. I even tried to organize a support group in Columbus because I felt so much pain and needed support. TN is the disease which causes more suicides than any other.

The pain was unbearable, and I finally had an episode in the neurologist's office, at which point he hurried out of the room and gave me a prescription to go to Cleveland Clinic. My son drove me there, and the doctor I saw told me, in no uncertain terms, that I had cancer and needed a biopsy to determine if it was malignant or not.

I tried to sue the neurologist, but I could not find an attorney to take my case. In Ohio, the doctors and attorneys hold hands together against malpractice cases. When I was told I had cancer, I was almost relieved.

I knew something could be done about cancer. On the way home from Cleveland, I hurt so badly that I curled up into the fetal position, and as Robert was pulling onto the freeway to get back to Columbus, I almost opened the door to just roll out. But I didn't!

The doctor in Cleveland made an appointment for me with Dr. David Schuller, a well-known cancer surgeon at the James Cancer Clinic at Ohio State University. My son had to put his knee on my chest to keep me still while they took a biopsy without using any sedative. The biopsy was malignant, my family was called, and I had surgery four days later. It turned out that the cancer was growing up my trigeminal nerve. It came within millimeters of reaching my brain. If it had reached my brain, there would have been very little that could have been done.

Probably the worst part of the whole ordeal was three nurses trying to perform a spinal tap. I was on a gurney, ready to be rolled into the MRI machine—a machine that I think was made in hell and delivered personally by the devil himself. They tried eleven times to get a spinal tap, and finally they just gave up. I peed, my bowels moved, I cried, and all the innocent nurses kept saying, "You're doing fine. It's okay." Finally they cleaned me up and put me into the MRI. Right at that moment, I lost every ounce of dignity I ever had. My body was no longer a "temple." From that time forward, I will show my butt to any doctor or nurse who wants to see it!

After surgery, I stayed in the hospital ten days and ten more in a rehab center. It reminded me of the mental institution I had to stay in when I was younger. I was a model patient and did everything they asked me to do so I could go home. I was released ten days later.

But while I was in the hospital after surgery, they gave me Dilaudid for pain; I found out I am extremely allergic to Dilaudid. For four nights, I was paranoid and schizophrenic. The first night, I walked the halls naked and found things the hospital didn't even know were there – like nurses' homes with garages. They caught me and tied me down in bed. Being so little, I unhooked all the tubes, wriggled under the ties, and again walked the halls naked. They thought I was a nut case, and it never occurred to my older sister who stayed with me or to my son to tell them that I didn't act like this normally. The hospital hired a babysitter to stay with me the rest of the night.

On the second night, I saw two mice come up out of the sink drain; one had on a top hat and was wearing a tuxedo. It carried a cane and danced and sang songs from the 1930s. The other was just a plain brown mouse. I'm scared to death of mice, so I started throwing everything I could at them. I made so much noise that a nurse came in. She said, "Okay," and she ran out to get a doctor.

The third night I solved a murder mystery. It was a complicated story involving a U.S. Senator from Alaska. I rang the buzzer for the nurse and told her quietly, as if we might be overheard, that if she would just look in the closet, she would find the evidence. She just replied, "that's okay sweetie."

On the fourth and last night, I called my son at three a.m. in a panic. I said, "Where are you? The planes are parked right outside my window, and we need to be on them to get to New York in time." In time for what, I don't know. That was the last straw. My son came over and told the doctor that something was very wrong. They changed my pain medicine to Roxicet, a liquid Percocet, and I returned to normalcy. Roxicet is still my drug of choice today for pain medication.

When I left the hospital in a wheelchair, the head nurse leaned down to me, winked, and said, "I won't tell anybody, if you won't!" I received a letter of apology from the hospital. I left the hospital with spinal meningitis (*duh!*), and my friend and caregiver had to gravity-feed me antibiotics through my Medi-port several times a day.

They thought they had gotten all of the cancer, and they tried to save my right eye, but a year later to the month, my cancer came back. Before that time, I had several more operations to try to give my right eye the ability to close. And the skin graft above my eye wasn't healing either. They were going to do another surgery, but instead they decided to give me Peacock Stereoscopic Radiation, which would reach the specific area needed to prepare for use after the surgery. For this, I had four holes drilled into my skull, which was then anchored with screws. These screws would be attached to a machine to keep my head perfectly still. This way they could give me high doses of radiation without killing healthy cells. I had to wear a cap to cover the screws sticking out of my head while my skull healed, and they gave me a black patch to wear over my right eye.

The hope was that the cancer had not reached my brain. This time, the doctors performed a complete right face maxillectomy, and I lost my right eye. But the good news was, with all the prayers that were being said for me, the cancer stopped in the minute space between the skull and the brain.

This time my face was really disfigured, and with my patch over my eye, little kids at Walmart would say, "Look, mommy, a pirate!" I would tell them that my ship was parked right outside the store. Later I got glasses with the right side blackened out.

So far, for four years, I have been cancer - free. It hasn't been all that easy however, because the radiation and chemotherapy I received are still causing problems. For example, I don't have enough saliva to swallow and have to suck on Halls cough drops all day and night or my mouth gets completely dry. I also have to gag up the saliva because it doesn't go all the way down and just builds up layer after layer. I eat only liquids through a feeding tube and have to crush up all of my solid medicines so they can go down my tube. I cannot swallow anything but tiny sips of water, which often come right out my nose. I thought that once I was diagnosed with no cancer that I would just get better and better. But I found out that's not usually the way it works due to the continual damage caused by chemotherapy and radiation.

I was uncomfortable with the stares I would get from people. So I decided to buy some tee shirts with slogans on them. Right now I have three. They say:

"Hug me I'm not contagious; I just have cancer."

"This is what a cancer survivor looks like."

"I don't need no diagnosis to fight cancer."

I find that the tee shirts make people feel more comfortable—some smile and others actually do hug me.

Probably my biggest concern is my ability to be understood, particularly on the phone. My speech gets worse when I get tired, and some people are just better at understanding me than are others. I was on the Board of Directors at the high-rise condominium building where I now live, but I had to remove myself because people couldn't understand what I was saying. I don't want to lose communication with what's left of our large family. My cancer has brought them closer to me.

I have two funny stories to tell before I move on. The first has to do with what exactly I was gagging up. They looked just like fishing worms. I put them under a magnifying glass with good light to see if they were moving. I explained this to Dr. Teknos, my second surgeon, who has a sense of humor. He just brushed off my concerns.

But then I watched an episode of *Animal Planet* entitled "The Things Inside of Us," and I knew I definitely had worms. To satisfy me, Dr. Teknos asked me to bring in a sample, and he agreed to check them out. I froze a sample, and when Dr. Teknos saw them, he just laughed. He said, "You've been watching too much *Animal Planet!*" We both had a good laugh.

The other story happened recently when I had to go to the emergency room at OSU, and I called my son, who had on his Highway Patrol uniform, complete with gun, a taser gun, and a pair of handcuffs because he was on his way to work. But he turned right around and drove me to the OSU emergency room. I noticed everyone looking at us, but Robert just smiled.

When we registered, the nurse asked Robert, "So, this is your prisoner?"

Of course I was absolutely offended and said, "I'm not a prisoner; I got my master's degree at this university…" and I went on and on. But Robert just sat there with his arms folded and with a grin on his face, calm as a cucumber, and after I calmed down, he said, "No ma'am; this is my dad." She apologized.

Well, we were in the waiting room quite a while, and I got up a few times and used the bathroom while Robert moved around to stretch his legs. And every time, people stared at us. Finally, one of the black male attendants took Robert aside and said, "I see the man you're with get up and go to the bathroom on his own, and you move around and get food. Aren't you afraid he might escape?" Robert laughed and said, "No, sir; that's my dad." The two then high fived, and I got the best treatment one could get in an emergency room!

Chapter 11
MY INNER FEELINGS
ABOUT BEING GAY

As I read my before "I-turned-it-in manuscript," it was evident to me that I had not written enough about my personal feelings about growing up gay in this era. Because of this, I have added another chapter to do just that.

There is no doubt that growing up gay in the years before the Stonewall uprising was very different than it is today. Younger gay people today should rejoice that there are so many gay organizations, legal victories, PFLAG organizations, and more, which make gay life easier than it was sixty years ago. We may not be where we need to be in terms of equality, and there are still many more battles to be fought and won, but we are definitely in a better place.

When I was young, before I fully understood what being gay was all about, I was constantly haunted by the fact that I knew I was different, even if I didn't know what to call it. Not a day passed when I didn't think about this difference. I continually asked myself, *Why me? How is this going to affect my life in the present, near future, and in the big picture? What if I am discovered for my difference? Could I go to jail? Could my parents disown me? What will my siblings think?* These kinds of questions and concerns were part of my everyday life.

I never felt like I belonged to any group, not even my family. In church groups, as I got older, I pretended that what older people said applied to me, too, but inside, I knew in many ways it didn't. I felt alone even in groups of people my own age because I knew I didn't fully share their interests. I felt detached and always on pins and needles as if someone would see me for what I was.

I became very distrustful of people and I didn't want to let them get too close; I built up a wall around me so no intruder could get in. I felt as though I was just going through the motions of living. I can't say that I wasn't frightened; there were times when I was very afraid I would say the wrong thing at the wrong time and give myself away. Being gay became a well-guarded secret.

As I got older, when I was ten to twelve years of age, I began wondering who else might be gay. I knew from adults that sexual perversion often meant being effeminate, so I was constantly on the lookout for feminine-looking or feminine-acting men. I was sorely afraid I would become feminine as the years unfolded. This scared me.

I remember one incident when I was about eleven years old; I had a crush on one of my male classmates. He lived in a house right next to our church, and I could look out of the window of the church into his house. I always tried to sit where I had the best view, and the highlight of the evening church service for me was when I could catch a glimpse of this boy. But at the same time, I was afraid that my parents would wonder why I always wanted to sit in this exact pew. It was during this time that I longed to have someone to talk to—I kept everything bottled up inside and felt sometimes as if I could explode.

After I inadvertently came out to my parents, I thought I would be able to talk to them about some of my feelings. However, the way my parents handled these kinds of problems was to be silent. I felt as if I had opened one door only to have another slammed in my face. In retrospect, I don't think they knew what to say. In that era, it was a pretty closed topic for discussion. That's when my mother's attention focused on changing me into a heterosexual so I could go to Heaven. In a way, I think that solved her dilemma regarding addressing the issue. I think she used her contention of my becoming heterosexual as a crutch to avoid a conversation she couldn't handle. This is when I realized there is a big difference between being tolerated and being unconditionally accepted.

I felt keenly left out when every other boy my age was dating. I couldn't share my 'hustling' experiences, nor did I want to, which again left me out of things. I often stayed home alone on Friday and Saturday nights, and would play the piano for hours, but I longed for a relationship of my own. I just didn't know how to go about finding anyone I could connect with. I tried to date girls, but I felt empty inside.

When I found out there were gay bars, I became obsessed with finding them, and when I did, it created a whole new set of problems. This was the beginning of the AIDS epidemic, and there were many aspersions cast in the media about gays. I read articles about bathhouses being shut down, even though I didn't know what a bathhouse was. All of this negative attention toward gays caused me to have negative feelings toward myself. This resulted in my inability to trust anyone who was gay. The more I knew about AIDS, the more frightened I became, and I was quickly reminded of my hustling days. I quietly made an appointment to get tested for AIDS with a doctor unknown to my family. I prayed a lot during the waiting period for the results of the test. When they came back negative, I vowed I would never knowingly put myself in any situation where I could contract the AIDS virus.

I disagreed with many of the behaviors that gay people were exhibiting during this time. Why did gay men put themselves at risk just for a one-night stand? There was a lot of this kind of behavior when I first went to gay bars in Chicago—not only risky sexual behavior but also illegal drugs, pill-popping, and excessive drinking. It seemed to me that most gay people just wanted to let loose on the weekends, and the bars were the places to do it. All I wanted was companionship and somebody to love and be loved by.

When Norm, my sister's ex-boyfriend, and I split up and I tried to commit suicide, I felt cheated; this was my first relationship, and I just believed it should and would last forever. As I look back after all these years, I think it was really puppy love and I was trying to live in an ideal dream world that didn't exist. If it hadn't been for my youngest sister, Karen, who was a psychiatric nurse and who understood and accepted what gay life was all about, I'm not sure I would have had the resolve to pick myself up or get back up after my failed suicide attempt. Karen was totally non-judgmental, and I discovered I had at least one family member who empathized with me. She and I became very close after this and shared many personal moments in our lives with each other.

Being gay was no easy thing, even in the 1970s through the 1990s. It largely depended on what part of the country you lived in and what your occupation was. I had two strikes against me: I moved to Ohio, a very conservative state, and my occupation was teaching in middle school. Even though my "gaydar" wasn't very good, I quickly learned whom I could and couldn't trust.

Everything I did carried the umbrella of being gay over it. When I taught, I put my whole self into it. Nothing distracted me, but even so, there were some rough times. For example, I had to park my car quite a distance from any gay bar I went to so students and teachers wouldn't recognize my car. (Of course that's all changed now.)

In the teachers' lounge, I made sure I crossed my legs properly; if I knew I had a gay student in class who was mixed up and was reaching out for help, I could do nothing to help. I remember one time I had a very effeminate student in class who was not only picked on by students, but by the school counselor as well. She tried to force exercises on him to make him "more manly," she told me. Fortunately, his mother knew and accepted her son, and when she found out what was going on, she came to the school and told the counselor, in no uncertain terms, to leave her child alone!

Although I couldn't say anything, I decided to take matters into my own hands. I had one of the star basketball players tutor this particular student, and out of respect for the basketball player, students pretty much stopped bullying him. His mother thanked me, although we never talked about the reason behind this.

This was a time in Ohio when I saw many gay people lose their jobs simply because they were gay. It quite often happened particularly to naïve gay people who weren't used to going to bars and tried to meet other gay people in inappropriate ways. One of the things I have always been thankful for was the fact that my relationships were long-term, and as I watched people die from AIDS all around me, I was spared this fate.

When Gary and I moved into a new neighborhood where we were restoring a home, I was always very cautious. Some neighbors were nosey and tried to get into our business by asking us inappropriate questions; others just accepted us for who we were without question. We made many friends over the years, and perhaps we made a few enemies as well. I always appreciated Gary's outgoing personality – you couldn't help but like him!

But there were incidents that happened that were truly biased and hurtful. My favorite home that we restored, the 1803 brick colonial (see picture), was put into a hardbound book highlighting the historical homes in Fairfield County. This was done by the local heritage society. Although we worked harder on this house than any other, the author left our names out completely. She mentioned the previous owner's names and later owner's names, but not ours. She knew what she was doing, and it hurt us. Had we not bought the home and restored it, it probably wouldn't be standing today.

But in another home, in another county, the local historical society asked us if they could hold their next meeting at our house. We felt honored. It just depended on the biases of different people; some could and would make our lives easier, and some could and would make our lives more difficult.

After I had tried to commit suicide and luckily failed, I met another one of my younger sister's college boyfriends. He wrote me a letter and said he had heard that I was gay. He asked if he could visit me in Columbus. I agreed, and he came and immediately fell in love with me. However, I didn't feel the same way about him; he just wasn't my type. But because I had just broken up with Norm and remembered how that had made me feel, I was really reluctant to tell him my true feelings and hurt him the same way that I had been hurt. When I finally did, he cried, I cried, and I'm not sure who felt worse. He moved to Germany permanently to live, and I've not heard from him since.

Another time I met man at a bar who was younger than I was, and we dated for a while without any sexual contact. I didn't realize he was falling in love with me. When he told me this, I didn't feel the same way about him. We broke up one weekend, and the next weekend he was shot and killed over a pool-game argument in the same bar where we had met. I decided to take it very slow after these two incidents. Life has its strange quirks! And in some ways, I decided being gay could be risky.

When you grew up gay in my era, you could never relax nor could you remove the albatross from around your neck. People who are closed-minded and bigoted, who want you to live your life just like theirs, can make your life constantly stressful. Some will use any means necessary, including quoting the Bible to try to make your life miserable. "Judge not, lest ye be judged," (Matthew 7, verse 1, The Schofield Reference Edition), has no meaning for these people. And in the end, I guess I just feel sorry for them.

Gay people have come a long way, thanks to those who have been willing to fight on all levels, but my gay and transgendered brothers and sisters have a long ways to go. When our U.S. Constitution will eventually have the same meaning for everyone, including all minorities, then I think being gay will no longer be an issue. Right now, gay rights are being fought for, with some successes and some disappointments, in every state and at every legislative level. The fight will continue, and right now I'm happy to share in this fight in my small way!

Chapter 12
WHERE WE ARE NOW, SOME HISTORY AND UPDATES

ME **(Bernie)** - I was born on December 3, 1943, in Brocton, New York, in the same hospital that Lucille Ball was born in. It was during a blizzard. We lived high up on a hill in a farmhouse. The snow was so deep my father couldn't drive the car up the hill and left it at the bottom. My mom went into labor and was just about to give birth, but my father was milking the cows in the barn and couldn't hear her. My mother banged two pans together to get my dad's attention, a signal they had worked out earlier. Dad harnessed the horses to a sleigh and took my mother to the hospital, where she delivered a barely five-pound boy. I was such a tiny baby, that I was taken home in a shoebox.

Sixty-eight years later, and in my fifth year of being cancer - free, I, however, am still feeling the effects of radiation and chemotherapy. I pretty much have to keep to a daily routine: "eating" three cans of food per day through my G-tube, taking daily medicine in the morning and at night, taking pain medicine every four hours or as needed, changing my oral prosthesis, usually two times a day, changing my gauze padding around my feeding tube daily, changing my eye bandage every three days where the skin graft didn't heal properly, putting medicine on my feet for neuropathy caused by radiation and chemotherapy, reading my daily devotional book, keeping doctors' appointments, shaving, bathing, and going to bed with a little TV here and there. Oh, and I also do two crossword puzzles daily to keep my mind young! There isn't much "me" time—then again, maybe it's all "me" time!

I still love to collect antiques, particularly Ohio pottery and old Delft. But I don't get out to too many auctions these days. My favorites to collect are Rookwood and Weller, of which I have quite a collection.

My son, Robert, lives about fifteen minutes away in Berwick, a Columbus suburb. I see him often, and we call each other several times a week.

It's getting more and more difficult to keep up my condo, which is lovely but too large. I would like to find something smaller, but I'm not able to do restoration work like I used to—and the thought of packing everything—*ugh*! I put two mattresses on the floor in the TV room because I had this strange fear of dying alone in my back bedroom. I asked Dr. Teknos, my cancer surgeon, how and when I would die (I was looking for a prognosis), but he laughed and told me he didn't think I would ever die with my sense of humor. He told me, "I don't know what you do, but whatever it is, keep doing it!" Both my sister and brother died exactly three years after they were diagnosed with cancer. I plan to live many more years. I haven't even had my carpet cleaned yet!

So far, I have cost my insurance and Medicare over two million dollars, and my medical prescriptions run around forty thousand dollars each year. Every year, Columbus has a Susan G. Komen Race for the Cure, a marathon that raises money for cancer research. Motorcycles line up on both sides of the street, and the bikers rev up their engines at the start of the race. Robert owns a pristine Harley Davidson that he had custom made just for him. I think we would like to be in the next race (I'll walk) and take my granddaughter, Aliya, with me to lean on when I get tired. Aliya is nine years old and beautiful. (I can say that because she's mine!) I don't think she would mind if I leaned on her the last mile or so. She loves the little presents I save for her and give to her for no particular occasion. She is in fourth grade and goes to a Catholic school. Every now and then she will call me and since she can't understand me very well, hands the phone to her dad.

When I retired from the Columbus Public School System, Mara and another wonderful friend, Jan, took charge of the retirement party. For some reason, I was fearful that no one would come. Mara sent out invitations. I kept asking her how many people had responded, and she would say, "Nobody yet." The closer the party came, the more nervous I got. Mara had reserved a large dining room at nice restaurant. A couple of days before the party, I asked her again, and she said a few had RSVP'd. I could just see it now—Mara, Jan, two others, and me sitting at one huge table all alone!

Well, to my surprise when I walked in, the place was decorated beautifully, and there were about a hundred and fifty teachers—some of whom I hadn't seen in years. My mother, my youngest sister, and my son were there also. One of my favorite teachers, Michelle, got up to speak, and she made a beautiful presentation that made me cry. I tried not to, but couldn't help it. Then my sister spoke and told some of the funny stories she remembered from when we were kids growing up.

Finally, Robert got up to speak. I had never heard Robert give any speech, and I was kind of nervous and didn't know what to expect. But he spoke with strong confidence in his voice and said, "Some of you may call our guest Mr. Martin; some of you may call him Bernie; some of you may call him boss; but I'm the only one who gets to call him Dad!" There wasn't a dry eye in the house.

I still want to see one more gay pride parade; this year there were over two hundred thousand in the parade, including onlookers. I'm always saddened by one float that carries many teenagers whose parents have kicked them out of the house upon learning they are gay. Columbus has a safe haven for them. But I'm proud to see so many PFLAG mothers and fathers supporting their gay children and marching along beside them.

There seems to be no end to my doctor appointments. Right now I'm in speech therapy to teach me to swallow easier and to be understood better. My prosthesis makes it difficult for family members to understand me on the phone. If I'm not going to have my Medi-ports flushed, then I'm going to have my feeding tube replaced. It's always something! I live on Roxicet, and it takes care of most of my pain. I have a live-in friend and caregiver, Marvin, and he helps. He's strong and tall and can lift things that I can't. Sometimes when I get lonely, I think of all the good memories I've had, and I've had many. I miss my younger sister, Karen.

I'm okay with dying, but I feel like I have a lot more living left to do. I need to see how my two grandchildren turn out. And, I still need to be there for Robert. He still needs and wants my acceptance, although I've told him he really doesn't need my opinion anymore and that I'm already proud of him. Jessie and I stayed together for twenty-two years, and by any gay person's standards, I have been lucky. I've had three long-term relationships. I'm content to be alone now.

Robert Martin – After Robert moved out, his life was a little topsy-turvy. He moved in with his grandmother for three weeks, and then he moved in with his girlfriend. During this time, he was driving his old truck to work at Taco Bell three miles away, but it was winter, and the temperature was below zero, and his truck wouldn't start. So, he walked all the way to Taco Bell, knowing he would be late but hoping to be forgiven under the circumstances. When he got there, the young, white manager said, almost like she was enjoying it, "You're fired for being late!" (I'm sure she will go a long way!) He had to walk the whole way back. I wish he'd told me about that when it happened, but he didn't.

After working as a bouncer in a few clubs, Robert went to the Columbus Police Academy and got his certification to become a police officer. He became a security guard at Lazarus. After a while, he decided he'd had enough low-paying jobs, and without any financial help from me, went back to college. He went to Columbus State Community College and transferred his credits to the Ohio Dominican College, where he graduated with a degree in law enforcement.

He worked as an internal investigator for The Limited Company and was paid well. Every Monday, he travelled by plane to some city in his territory where there was a suspicious loss at one of The Limited stores. He would interrogate suspects, etc., and then he would return home by Friday. While he worked for The Limited, he would pull extra duties for the Whitehall Police Department. With the two salaries combined he made close to, and sometimes over, ninety thousand dollars—more than his dad ever made!

At an auction, Robert and I bid on a home for him to live in. We won and went right to work on it. It just needed some updating. He moved two of his friends in with him to help pay for the mortgage. After a few years, we sold the house for quite a profit. I had gotten my realtor's license because I was turning over so many homes and I didn't want to pay realtor fees anymore. Then we had enough money to buy a cute home in a better neighborhood. He decided to settle down, get married, and have a family. He had waited a long time; a lot of his friends had already married, and some were even divorced and single again.

He met a woman at his bank; she was from the Dominican Republic. They dated awhile, and she became pregnant. I, of course, wanted them to be married before the baby was born. They were married in the Franklin Park Conservatory right across the street from my condo, and the reception was held in the Social Room at my condo. It was a beautiful event. I wasn't sure if Robert was going to get out the words, "I do," but eventually he did.

They had one child, Aliya, and then a second, Haven, a son, two years later. Their first language is Spanish, and their second is English. The marriage didn't work out, and they were divorced; they have shared custody of their children, but Robert has them most of the time. In fact, he quit his job at The Limited and took a huge pay cut just so he could spend more time with his children. He is a wonderful father. Haven has some developmental problems and has a one to one teaching/learning situation.

With my cancer, I haven't been able to see them as much as I would like. After each surgery, the doctors remind me to stay away from school-age children so I won't pick up any of their infections, which could be dangerous for me. Robert has been very good to me during this very difficult time. Even though I can still drive, I don't feel safe, so he or my caregiver take me to most of my doctor appointments.

That one awful principal told me he didn't think it was a good idea for me to adopt Robert. I'm so glad I listened to my own head and heart. Adopting Robert is the best decision I've made. Not too many gay couples who have children know that I helped forged the way. Robert has been with me to a few gay bars, where we would mostly shoot a game of pool.

What is fascinating to me is that the Martin name will change from all white to all black. I have only two nephews who could carry on the Martin name, but it looks doubtful that they will.

Aliya – Robert's daughter is rather shy around me and has a hard time understanding me. I always take her Christmas shopping so she can purchase presents for others in her life. I want her to learn that Christmas isn't only about receiving gifts, but giving them as well. The first time we went shopping, she thought they were all for her, and I think she was a little disappointed until she saw how others reacted getting her gifts. Now I think she looks forward to it. I let her choose the paper, and write her name on the name tabs – it takes most of the day! She is in the fourth grade and is a pretty good student. I wish I had more chances to see her, but my fighting cancer can get in the way.

Haven - Robert's son is seven years old and he looks like Robert just "spit him out." He is very much into computers. As soon as he comes home from school, he runs to the computer! He probably could have formatted this book quicker than I could!

Bernard Cecil Martin –My father was the hardest-working man I've ever known. He worked night and day; with a family of six children and wanting every one of them to graduate from college, he had no choice. He made us work hard too. I appreciate him for that. His father was quite wealthy and owned the only car in Aberdeen, North Dakota. But he crashed it into a tree and killed himself when my father was only twelve years old. My dad and his mother would go to school dances together, and nobody could tell the age difference. His favorite sport was tennis, and he was state champion of North Dakota. I loved and respected my dad for all his hard work. He never asked for anything himself. Every business he ever tried seemed to fail, and then when the bill collectors would call, Mom would turn to me to talk about my dad. For a while, I didn't think she loved him as much as he loved her. He would ask my Mom what she wanted for Christmas, and she would say, "Nothing. We have enough expenses as it is." Then when Christmas came and she didn't have a present from him, she would cry or get into a mood and spoil the day for the rest of us. We finally took my dad aside and told him not to ask her anymore. Just buy her a present!

But I guess Mom really did love Dad. She took round-the-clock care of him when he had sugar diabetes and lost a toe that wouldn't heal. It eventually led to a stroke and then to his death. My dad never touched me affectionately, only with a belt over his knee. When he lay dying in the hospital, all of us children came home and took turns being with him. It was a terrible death; his organs shut down, one after the other.

I wrote earlier that my father didn't stick around to listen to my mom insist that I was going to hell if I didn't become heterosexual. I found out why. When it was my turn to watch my father, he could barely whisper and was just hours away from dying. He motioned me over and grabbed my hand, which surprised me. He pulled me down and whispered, "You're all right." I intuitively knew what he meant. I didn't cry at his funeral, but two weeks later, it just hit me at work, and I started crying. They sent me home. Dad didn't pass until my sister said it was okay for him to go, and then he just slipped away.

Three months later, I was driving my car when I looked in the rearview mirror, and there was my dad, sitting in the back seat. He said, "You're going to be okay." I looked back again, and he was gone. Again, I intuitively knew what he meant. I was going to Heaven as a gay man.

I thought I was crazy and didn't tell anyone about this for close to six months. Then one day, my younger sister and I were taking a walk in the woods. We were talking about family and Dad's death, and I shared with her my experience with Dad while driving. Karen's mouth dropped, and she said, "When was this?" She kept trying to get me to tell her the exact date. I asked her why this was so important, and she started to cry. She told me that Dad had appeared to her the same way and said the exact same words to her. We felt spooked. But I believe to this day, my dad was sent back to earth to let us know that we would go to Heaven some day. And for me, I no longer cared what my mom said about going to hell. He died at age eighty-four in 1991. I miss him!

Isabelle Yvonne Martin —My mom lived to be ninety-four; all of her siblings lived a very long life. The ones who died were all in their eighties and nineties. The four who are left are all in their nineties. My Aunt Dottie will be ninety-seven on July 30, 2012. But my mom, like one of her sisters, developed Alzheimer's and went through every dreadful stage of the disease. We first noticed something was wrong when she made only right turns to go to the store or to church. When we asked her why, she said she felt safer because she didn't have to make any left turns! She was in her late eighties by then. We knew she shouldn't be driving, but she didn't want to lose her independence. When she shopped, she would buy just nine string green beans—just enough for herself!

My sister decided to take her to renew her license, hoping she would fail the test. Karen let Mom drive there, and she had no fear that she wouldn't pass the test. Mom crept up to a stop sign, and without looking in either direction, she shot through the intersection as if she were late to a fire! The man who took Mom out for her driving test came back shaking and pale. Needless to say, Mom didn't pass the test. She called all of us together because she had an announcement to make. I was expecting the worst news. But she said, "I didn't pass my driving test, and I won't be driving anymore." And the tears came to her eyes. We all rejoiced inside. It didn't stop her, however, when she was in her late eighties, from climbing a ladder with gloves on and a bucket of tar to repair a leak in the roof. She finally had to give up her home and move into a beautiful retirement center with assisted living facilities.

She didn't know any of us the last couple of years. My sister, Ann, who lived closest to her, saw her the most and gave her the most care. One day, my mom hid behind doors naked and "flicked" other patients passing by with a wet towel. She would grin just like a devilish young child. One of the last times I saw her was on her last birthday. Ann had bought her a cake, and my mother put her face down into the cake and started eating it. She no longer knew what her eating utensils were for. This was hard to comprehend. She had graduated as valedictorian of her high school class and graduated from Greenville Free Methodist College with straight A's.

My mother died on May 24, twenty-five days before my brother died of brain cancer. When Mom died, all my siblings spoke at her funeral. But I wasn't in a forgiving mood yet, so I didn't speak. I'm sorry we couldn't agree on my lifestyle, but as I wrote earlier, maybe we can sort it all out in heaven.

Karen White – My youngest sister, Karen, and I were the closest of all our siblings. She married and had one daughter. Her husband was abusive, and the marriage lasted only three years. Karen was a single mother for the rest of her life. One thing I will never forget about Karen, besides conking me in the head in the dump when we were younger and knocking me out, was that she refused to die of cancer before she could see her daughter marry. She made it to the wedding—didn't look good—but she made it!

She declined precipitously after her daughter got married, but Robert's wedding was going to be in three weeks, and Karen called me and said she _would_ be there for the wedding! I tried to convince her not to come, as the drive from Indiana would be difficult for her. After all the wedding guests were seated, I didn't see any sign of Karen. And then, right before the wedding march started to play, Amanda, Karen's daughter, wheeled her down the center aisle right up to the front next to me. We cried and hugged. By this time, cancer had spread throughout her entire body. It took two strong men to lift her gently into the car to go home.

She said she wanted to be there for Robert's wedding, and she hung on until she did! She died a week later, alone in hospice. I miss her very much! Her daughter is now living in Italy working on her MA degree.

Glenn Martin – My brother, Glenn, always had an opinion about everything, and he always thought he was right. He married a Southern woman and had three wonderful children and six grandchildren. The best way to describe Glenn is to describe his funeral. He was Dean of the History Department at Indiana Wesleyan University. He had brain cancer but taught and worked on his book up until a month before he went into the hospital. When I visited him, he had knots that stuck out of his head, and his forehead had pushed outward. Karen's brain cancer didn't show. Anyway, Glenn's casket was open, but all the bumps were gone, thanks to some very good work by the embalmer. I wish to be cremated—I don't want anyone to remember me with half a face—and they can have a memorial service afterward.

But back to Glenn's funeral. He was a popular professor and had friends all over the world. The church where his funeral was held was the college church, which was huge. I'd never been to a more formal funeral. At this funeral, family members came in after everyone else was seated, and we had front row pews tied off with ribbons. All the people stood as we entered down the center aisle. Next came the funeral procession—the pallbearers carried the casket high—and they were dressed in tuxedos. There were hundreds of people there. This is the way he lived his life, and it was the way he passed out of it too. One speaker said Glenn never complained once about all the pain he was in. I honor him for this.

Ann Moore – My oldest sister, Ann, has had a wonderful life; she never needed a job for financial reasons, and she had the chance to raise three wonderful children. It wasn't all roses, though. Bob, her husband, is six feet tall, and Ann is a little over five feet tall. She takes after my mom's side of the family as we all did except for Karen, who took after Dad's side of the family. When Ann had her first child, he was a big baby, and he cracked Ann's tailbone during delivery. Pam, her second child, also took after her father, and this time Ann's tailbone was totally broken. But she did have a third child and has many grandchildren who are now in college or getting married.

She has suffered from back pain all her life. She went through a series of doctors who tried different things, but Ann never found any real relief. Recently, though, she had laser surgery and has great hopes for success. She's still going through the healing process.

I didn't know Ann that well as a child, as she was already in college when I remember her. She even played with a whole different generation of cousins than I did. She got married before any of Dad's financial crises hit the younger children. But both she and Bob loved my mother and took good care of her, and for that I am grateful. They also have been very good to me during my illness, stopping in from Elkhart or Florida to bring me wonderful books to read. I thank them for that.

I wasn't sure how Ann and Bob felt about my being gay until we had a discussion about where I stood with my faith in God. They no longer shared my mother's beliefs about twenty years ago, and I didn't know that. It makes it more fun to talk with them now.

Mary Smith – My older sister, Mary, was more naïve and shyer than Ann. Mary's beliefs are very similar to Mom's, and she has never altered them much to this day. But she and her husband, Tim, are very much in love with each other. They raised three wonderful children whose children are going to college now. Mary had her hands full taking care of three children and teaching each year.

They both were outstanding teachers. Tim was given several awards for teaching chemistry and was well liked by his students. Mary was an elementary schoolteacher, and I used to listen to her complain about one or two students in her class who wouldn't pay attention. She taught in a more rural area. I longed to have her situation. My students wanted to throw things at me and swear, until they learned who the boss was. I taught inner-city, poor children, and that made a real difference.

Even though we may disagree on a few or even several things, we have agreed to disagree. Some things we just don't talk about. Both Mary and Tim have been wonderful to me during my illness. Mary lives closer to me than any other sibling, and she and Tim have been to every one of my major surgeries and stayed with me until they saw I was okay. I really appreciate the time they have spent with me. They go to a Christian camp in New York every summer, and usually they stop in on the way there and on the way back.

Marvin – My little brother, Marvin, was born when I was six years old, and when he was old enough to ride in a stroller, I used to take him everywhere with me. He was cute as a button. When he was three years old, I wanted to give Mom a picture of the two of us for Mother's Day. A man down the street was an amateur photographer and was digging out a basement under his house. He had rigged up this conveyor belt that you could shovel dirt onto, and it would come up and out into a wheelbarrow. I asked him if he would take a picture of Marvin and me for Mother's Day if I helped him shovel out his basement. So, every night after school for about two months I shoveled and shoveled. It didn't look like we made much of a dent in his operation.

On the day we were to get our pictures taken, I got Marvin all dressed up in his new cowboy shirt, put on a nice shirt and sweater for myself, and we sneaked out of the house. That photograph was one of my mother's favorites, and now it's one of mine too. I have it on a large windowsill in my condo. (see pictures)

Marvin and his wife have one son, Danny, who was quiet and a good-looking teenager. I haven't seen him in several years.

Mrs. Poindexter – Robert's grandmother, Mrs. Poindexter, was elderly and had fairly severe asthma when I first met her. I always felt she might have been pretty wild in her youth but mellowed with age. She was a Christian, which she let you know because she sold pies and donated the profits to the minister of her church.

However, something weird was going on. I bought glasses and tons of clothing for Boo, Robert's little brother, and yet every time we picked him up for the weekend, he would be dressed in old, dirty clothes. And we would buy him more. I think I bought William three pairs of glasses. I don't know what was really going on, but I think I might have an idea.

Robert loved his grandmother, but the older he got, the more he fought her rules. Robert loved football, and his grandmother wouldn't let him play. When I asked her why, she said she needed him to clean the floors.

She was always good to me, and we got along fine. We went to a small African-American church with her once, and I was in for quite a shock. The minister used volume rather than words to lift your spirits. I don't think he said more than thirty words, but said them over and over, each time louder and louder, and stretched the syllables of each word longer. Finally Aunt Edna, Mrs. Poindexter's aunt, got up and danced and "whooped it up." I was glad to get home. Mrs. Poindexter always talked about her gentlemen callers and always had a separate, clean room for them. I'm not sure what that was all about.

Robert and I literally watched Mrs. Poindexter die. It shook me up! To watch someone you know die because he or she can't get enough air into the lungs is devastating. I never spoke negatively about her to Robert because I respected their relationship. She was in her eighties when she died.

Boo or William (as we call him now) – Boo is Robert's little brother. He suffered from the effects of his mother's alcoholism. He was only two or three when I adopted Robert; he was a cute little thing with a big grin and ears to match. His ears had to be surgically pinned back. But he was a handful! He was hyperactive, and I think his picture is in the dictionary by that word. We took him to Indiana one time for Christmas. His hands were all over every instrument and dial on the dashboard. I finally had to slap his little hands before we had a car wreck.

When we got to my mother's, Boo just took command. He was about five years old. My sister's daughter, Amanda, was about four years old. They were playing in the basement when all of a sudden Amanda came running up the stairs screaming, "That black boy said he was going to beat my butt if I didn't give him something he wants to play with!" We didn't use language like that in our house, but we couldn't stop laughing. Robert felt embarrassed.

Then when the whole family was sitting around the Christmas tree, waiting to open presents, Boo went into turbo charge! He picked up every present, and though we showed him whose it was, he had it half unwrapped before he got to the person. That was the fastest Christmas gift exchange our family ever had.

When William got older, he was in and out of jails for no particular reason. He would sleep in someone's car to stay warm or loiter somewhere he wasn't wanted. One time he went to Cleveland and was put in jail for some reason. I called the jail and asked them to call me when they were going to let him out. I planned to come pick him up and bring him back home. I knew he would get into trouble again if they didn't call me. Sure enough, they let him out of jail in the middle of winter and with no money, and they didn't call me. Of course, William got caught sleeping in someone's car and went back to jail. I had to go to Cleveland and plead his case until they finally released him into my custody.

But the strangest thing happened; William got a white girl pregnant, changed his life around, had two more children, and is a perfect father. He doesn't even go anywhere were he might end up in trouble. Both Robert and I are really proud of him.

Jesteen- Robert's older sister, Jesteen, was my student in English, and she was a strong B student. I don't know her whole life situation, but I do know that Robert helps her out now and then and that she babysits his children at times. She has three grown children, an ex-husband, and a new grandchild.

Norm – I have not seen my first significant - other, Norm, since I tried to commit suicide, nor do I ever want to. I did hear from a mutual friend that he had adopted a black child who gave him lots of trouble. I also heard that he would like to talk to me. No thanks!

Gary –When Gary, my second lover, and I broke up, and shortly after he came back to reconcile with me, he soon after hooked up with another teacher. They were together for 22 years. I loaned them money for a down payment for a beautiful Georgian home with acreage and a nice barn. Gary restored the home and then began to raise quarter horses, something Gary had always wanted to do. They were to pay me back monthly. After a year went by and I received no money, I called his lover, and that's when I realized something was wrong. His lover told me that it wasn't his problem, and he had no intention of paying me back. It was quite a large sum of money, so I said, "Oh, yes it is your problem; I have a signed contract with your name on it." He just blew me off.

I called Gary and told him to make sure his name was on the deed because the house was worth a lot more after being restored. Gary had gone to closing and assured me his name was on the deed, but he would check to make sure. Gary found out that this so-called lover had not put Gary's name on the deed at all. Gary had to have it changed. I found out years later that Gary's lover was a mean alcoholic. He had refinanced the property to the hilt without Gary's knowledge; he did pay me back eventually, but he wrote me a really nasty letter with his last payment.

Gary had been physically and emotionally abused by this "jerk" for many years. In desperation, he sought counseling, and it was suggested that he leave this relationship at once before he got really hurt. He went online and found a wonderful friend and lover. He had to sneak some of his antiques and personal belongings to Ashland, North Carolina, where he now lives. Once again, he's the old Gary whom I knew and loved—happy and fun loving. We call each other and send e-mails back and forth all the time. I am so happy for him and his partner, Jack. His old lover calls him when he's drunk and asks him to come back!

Jessie – My third lover, Jessie, graduated from Ohio Dominican with a degree in education. Right now he is teaching middle school. He has a beautiful daughter who is ten years old. We were together for twenty-two years—some good times, some not so good. He's finding out that teaching isn't as easy as he thought it would be!

Gloria Still – Robert's Aunt Gloria died of a heroin overdose several years ago, shortly after the death of Robert's mother.

Latrisa Mae Lowery – Robert's mother, Latrisa, died suddenly. The police didn't do a very thorough investigation of her death. We don't really know if she was beaten to death or died of alcohol poisoning. Jesteen,

Robert, and William all had different fathers, and only William knew who his father was.

Dr. Teknos – A good cancer surgeon, Dr. Teknos performed my second major surgery. He always takes the time to listen to you even if you don't have worms! I see him now about every six months. He still has a good sense of humor and good bedside manners. I always feel better after seeing him.

Marvin – Marvin, not my brother, is still my friend and caregiver.

Ernie, Rosemary, Jim, Hope, Mara, Pat, and Nancy – These are all my co-workers when I was a reading coordinator. They are all intelligent and full of energy and enthusiasm for their work. I know Rosemary was well liked in Reading Recovery. Mara's husband, Ed, was a teacher but had to take disability leave to undergo a heart transplant. That was several years ago, and he's doing fine today. I learned a lot from Pat and Mara, as we worked so closely together. Ernie, my boss, retired a year before I did. Nancy was my coordinator when I was a teacher at Champion, and then we became coordinators together. She then became my supervisor in my last year as reading coordinator. She retired, but now has returned to the system in some capacity. I didn't have a lot of contact with Jim, but he's the one who gave me the job. He was always a perfect gentleman. I knew his wife better. She was an Elementary Reading Coordinator in the same office I worked in.

Bad Principal – He died a few years after he left the second school that was getting ready to file a grievance. He used to tell off-color and racial jokes in the teachers' lounge after the African-American teachers left the lounge; I finally stood up to him one day, and said, "Do you realize you may be offending other teachers with your jokes besides Black teachers?" We did not like each other! I usually try to find something nice to say about each person I meet, but I worked under him for fifteen years and can honestly say I can't find anything!

*The Martin tribe. Bottom row (left to right): Mary, Ann, Mom, and Dad.
Top row: Karen, Bernie, Marvin, and Glenn.*

The Martin tribe again, with all the in-laws: Bob, Tim, Carol, and Betty.

Robert's high school picture.

My favorite picture of Marvin, my little brother, and me, our gift to Mom on Mother's Day.

*The Royalton house, which was built in 1803, the same year
Ohio became a state. My favorite home that I had to leave.*

*The Somerset home of Senator Finck, where
we had the Christmas party.*

*My sister, Karen, who was determined to see her daughter,
Amanda, marry. She died just a few weeks later.*

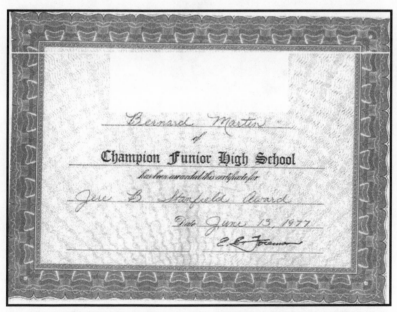

Bernard Martin

of

Champion Junior High School

has been awarded this certificate for

Jane B. Stanfield Award

Date June 13, 1977

*My "Teacher of the Year" Award, which I received in my third
year of teaching in a large, all-black middle school.*

My college picture.

My favorite picture of my grandchildren, Aliya and Haven. They are now nine and seven years of age.

My sister, Karen, when she was a practicing psychiatric nurse.

"Boo," or William, as we call him today.

Robert and me a few years after the adoption.

Robert feeding his firstborn, Aliya.
He's not too proud, is he?

The entire Morrison family: my mother's side of the family. My mother is on the bottom row, far right. Aunt Lil is second from the right in the top row.

Robert in his football jersey.

The condominium, where I live now.

Robert and his friends receiving their Police Certifications.

Robert with my mother and father.

Chapter 13
POINTS TO PONDER

- As a parent, study your children, know them, and let them tell and ask you anything, even if it upsets you.

- To the best of your ability, give age-appropriate, thoughtful answers to your child's early questions.

- To all gay, bisexual, lesbian, and transgendered people, don't be afraid to tell people who you are; let the chips fall where they may. If people cannot accept you, they are not worth the effort to build a relationship with anyway. You'll live a richer and happier life without them.

- Love your children unconditionally, including their sexual preferences and sexual identity. After all, that is a big part of their lives.

- Parents, don't blame yourselves for having a gay child. Get on the internet and find out how other parents are dealing with your same situation. Get in touch with a PFLAG organization. They're all over.

- It is not important or even worth coming out to all people.

- Gay people, please don't leave God out of your lives; remember, we too, are made in His image, and He wants us to lead full and happy lives.

- Parents don't lay guilt trips on your children about their sexual identities or preferences.

- Do not try to be something you're not; chances are you won't get away with it anyway. Even if you are gay and never have sex, you're still gay.

- Straight people, try to take risks with people different from yourselves, especially ethnically and sexually. You might find they're not so unlike yourself.

- When you love your children, love every part of them even if some parts feel unacceptable to you.

- Don't be so quick to judge gay people; statistically one might be a member of your family now or sometime in the future.

- If you are attending a church that doesn't accept gay people, you're going to the wrong church; God intended for places of worship to be open to everybody.

- Psychiatrists who think they can make gay people straight should try it on themselves first and see if they can become gay!

- Trying to be straight for the wrong reasons will not only hurt you, but also it will hurt others.

- If you find yourself in the position I was in as a young teen, take active steps to understand who you are; there's a lot of help out there now.

- Don't let family relationships die. They need nurturing, just like a plant, to grow and become strong.

- As you live your life, make sure you make good and happy memories – they may come in useful one day.

- Younger GLBTs need to know their history and not take for granted today's more accepting culture. Freedom should never be taken for granted because, in an instant, everything could change. It's important to show appreciation to older gays who have forged the way for younger gays to live more openly.

- And finally, learn to love and be loved – you're worth it!

LETTER TO ME FROM MY SON, ROBERT

Dear Dad,

As a young boy, thanks to certain mentors, I was able to develop to my full potential. One particular mentor was you, my father, Bernard Martin. You were an educational leader and an advocate for what is right. You saw so much potential in me that you took on the challenge of adopting me as your son.

Now I suspect, to most people, this seems simple, but it was not because you are a white man and I am black. While my grandmother taught me to respect adults, especially teachers, one of the most difficult but important lessons to learn as a black child was that I had to speak standardized English as well as the traditional black dialect of the streets—better known as Ebonics. More importantly, I had to know when to make that register switch.

As my father, you were able to see the potential in me, and you knew that I had the willingness to learn because of the strong effort I displayed in your classroom.

The turning point in my life was the death of my mother. I had already developed a relationship with you, my reading teacher, by then, due to the recent time I had spent with you during and after my mother's funeral. Because of our strong relationship, I asked you why you couldn't just adopt me so I could continue to grow and learn all the things I was missing from a biological father. You agreed and acknowledged that you would like to have a son. When you said yes, I was happy but afraid of the many cultural challenges we might face. I was also worried about having to go to a new school.

One of the first challenges I had to overcome was to improve my speech. This happened through reading regularly. I remember you used to bribe me and pay me a dollar for each book I had read. Also, because I was in a different environment, I was able to slowly get rid of the incorrect "he be" and "she be," which enabled me to speak standard English.

As my newly adopted father, you also shared with me and developed in me a sense of style, architecture, antiques, and landscaping. Even though sometimes I broke an antique or killed a bush, you took the time to make me appreciate the beauty and self-fulfillment of the things around us.

Dad, your trust in me was unconditional. You taught me to drive in your Mercedes, even though we had many close calls and even ran a few stop signs, which almost killed both of us!

One of the most unforgettable lessons you taught me was this: No matter what other people think or say, if you believe you are right, do not let others change your beliefs. That statement taught me to communicate with and educate the many narrow-minded people in my workplace and in my personal life. One such topic was whether or not to accept one's sexual orientation. You also taught me that the strength of intellect always trumps violence in any situation.

I want to thank you for all the effort you put into tutoring me and the lessons you've taught me. They have helped me many times in my work as an internal investigator for The Limited, and now as a highway patrolman. They continue to help me as I raise my own two children. I want to also thank you for your support when I played football. I know it was very cold on those bleachers sometimes, but I could always look up there and spot you! You have always been there for me when I've needed you.

I really can't put into words the feelings I have for you. Your love has made my life a much richer and fuller one. Thank you!

Sincerely, your son,

Robert Martin

AFTERWORD

THIS book turned out to be more emotionally difficult for me to write than I had imagined. It has been in my head for years, and the words spilled from my brain like lava flowing from a volcano. I started on a Tuesday and finished the following week on Wednesday. And I had two doctors' appointments in between!

The difficult part was reliving all the hurt, pain, and struggle I felt growing up. The difficult part was remembering those who went on before me; it was like reliving my family's deaths.

I cried several times while writing this book. I guess most people just store painful memories away and forget about them. When you write about them, it brings all the hurt back again.

The difficult part was that I know, if this book is published, I will have "outed" myself. The difficult part is that I may anger some of my friends or relatives who really don't know about my being gay. The difficult part is sharing something very personal with people who are my neighbors in the condominium complex where I live. The difficult part is in realizing there are a lot of people out there who will disagree with me. That's okay. They have a right to their opinions as long as they don't force their values on me or my gay brothers and sisters.

There has been a lot that has been difficult. But there has been an easy part too: this was a book that I felt had to be written. I've read about too many cases of gay suicides this past year because of harassment or because of a sense of unworthiness, and I have read about all the discrimination against gay, bisexual, lesbian, and transgender individuals who are still suffering from harassment and inequality.

I believe it's time for everyone, at least in America, where we hold such high standards about liberty and freedom, to understand that people do not choose their sexual identity. I also believe it's time for straight people to be more open-minded about the sexual preferences of others. Statistically, more than likely, they will need to be prepared to deal with a child, grandchild, niece, nephew, aunt, uncle, mother, father, husband, wife, butcher, baker, or candlestick maker who just happens to have a different sexual orientation from theirs. It is not our place to judge other people, and it is certainly not our place to discriminate against those who are different and to make their lives more difficult than they already are.

I hope I have communicated this message in telling about my own life experience. I appreciate the fact that so many others have stood up and shouted to the world that they are gay. We no longer have red lights in bars (Cat's Meow) that, when they came on, alerted us to when the police were coming to measure the distance between you and your dancing partner to determine if you had violated the law and needed to go to jail!

Things are slowly changing for gay people everywhere in America, and I'm glad to be part of that change. But there are still countries that put gay people to death, just like the Nazis did. The President of Iran announced that his country has no homosexuals! It took me sixty-eight years to come out of the closet, but I feel a sense of relief. I can now live my life the way I was meant to.